CONVERSIONS

LAURENCE KING

Published in 2007
by Laurence King Publishing Ltd
361-373 City Road
London
EC1V 1JJ
E-mail: enquiries@laurenceking.co.uk
www.laurenceking.co.uk

Text © Emma O'Kelly and Corinna Dean 2007
This book was produced by Laurence King Publishing Ltd

A catalogue record for this book is available from
the British Library.

ISBN-10: 1-85669-486-0
ISBN-13: 978-1-85669-486-5

Designed by Hoop Design

Printed in China

CONVERSIONS
Emma O'Kelly and Corinna Dean

LAURENCE KING PUBLISHING

CONTENTS

INTRODUCTION

CONVERTING OLD BUILDINGS into homes makes sense for many reasons. In cities, conversions are a means of recycling building stock and combating suburban sprawl. In rural areas, conversions can serve to regenerate depopulated areas. They also allow those who like the countryside, but not necessarily a rural aesthetic, to create more daring - even urban - architecture beyond the greenbelt.

In almost every instance, the conversion of an old building is an environmentally friendly, and often financially astute option. Why build from scratch when hundreds of derelict buildings are ripe for conversion? In this book we have searched the globe for the most inspired transformations of non-residential spaces into residential ones. We were strict about the criteria, which meant that we had to exclude many fine examples on the basis that they had not officially changed from one use to another. On our travels, it was easier to uncover projects in densely populated European countries than it was in North America, Australia, South Africa and parts of South America. We had to ask why. Do geographical factors such as plentiful land supply, low population density and an abundance of greenfield sites mean that these non-European countries are not pressured into recycling old building stock in the way that overcrowded parts of Europe are? Alternatively, conversions may be influenced by cultural factors whereby living in an ex-warehouse in the city or a former granary barn in the countryside speaks of a lifestyle choice, embedded in some cultures and absent in others?

Looking at cities such as New York, London and Berlin, where loft living was first seen as an option in the 1950s, we sought to discover whether these cites still contain the most evolved examples of residential conversions today. Examining the building types architects and city councils have deemed worthy of preservation, we witnessed that these change across cultures. In some, the idea of heritage architecture does not extend beyond the Victorian era, while in others it includes Modernist, industrial and post-Modernist buildings. Finally, we investigate a variety of quirky and eccentric conversions, finding that anything from former jet engines and sea containers, to missile silos and Martello towers can be turned into homes.

THE EVOLUTION OF LOFT LIVING

From its origins in 1950s New York, the concept of loft living has come a long way. What started out as a subversive movement by a group of avant-garde artists and bohemians had, by the 1990s, become the property developer's route to making a quick killing. Spaces that had been little more than squats with few amenities and original industrial

ROBERT MOTHERWELL IN HIS MANHATTAN LOFT STUDIO. ATTRACTED BY VAST SPACES AND LOW RENTS, MANY ARTISTS BEGAN MOVING INTO DISUSED INDUSTRIAL SPACES IN THE EARLY 1950s.

fittings, whose occupants railed against the suburban dream of a family house with garden and a car in the garage, evolved, at their worst, into poorly finished spaces with sky-high price tags, kitted out with a predictable list of furniture must-haves. Andy Warhol, Jean Michel Basquiat and other high-profile New Yorkers pioneered this new way of living only for urban professionals with healthy bank balances chasing a 'cool' lifestyle to follow.

At its best, however, the loft was - and still is - a showcase for experimental architecture, a smart form of urban living and a positive addition to many a deprived urban area. In the UK, developers such as the Manhattan Loft Corporation (MLC), founded by German-born, US-educated art collector and investor Harry Handelsman in 1992, and Manchester-based Urban Splash, founded by entrepreneur Tom Bloxham in 1993, spearheaded a new approach to development. They demanded a closer relationship between architect and developer, using design as a key selling point and adopting a canny marketing strategy that promoted loft living as a lifestyle choice. The message from MLC was that loft living gives the freedom to create a personal space and identity. Not

THE ARTIST LOWELL NESBITT LIVED AND WORKED IN THIS FORMER 1850s STABLE BUILDING IN NEW YORK'S GREENWICH VILLAGE, CONVERTED BY ARCHITECT EDWARD E. KNOWLES IN THE 1970s.

SUMMERS STREET LOFTS, A CONVERTED
PRINTWORKS IN LONDON'S
CLERKENWELL DISTRICT, WAS
MANHATTAN LOFT CORPORATION'S
FIRST RESIDENTIAL LOFT PROJECT.
DESIGNED BY PIERS GOUGH OF CZWG,
IT INCLUDES THREE COMMERCIAL
SPACES AND 25 APARTMENTS.

only can you be fashionable, cultured and daring, but also have the space for pinball machines, snooker tables, golf ranges and industrial appliances. It worked and people moved in droves from Victorian terraces to east London lofts developed by MLC. Urban Splash set about loft development in cities in northern Britain, including Manchester, Liverpool, Bradford and Leeds, remodelling huge post-industrial buildings into lofts and apartments, and repeating MLC's success in London.

THE POST-LOFT GENERATION

By the millennium, 1990s-style loft living, with its Bulthaup kitchens, Conran sofas and tick-the-box lists of mid-century modern furniture, was starting to become a cliché. Many people reverted to adding glass box extensions to their Victorian houses and exploring alternative urban sites such as churches, schools and water towers. However, MLC and its ilk had permanently changed perceptions about city living. Not only had open-plan living become widely popular but many people now had a new enthusiasm to personalize their living space, no matter where they lived.

'The loft movement was definitely a 1990s phenomenon, but it's still a fascination for young professionals. But the idea of what constitutes a loft has changed. The 1990s loft was an industrial warehouse space with large windows and a view onto a city skyline. Today the term has been twisted to incorporate a multitude of sins. It's a smaller flat with a double-height ceiling above the living room, a chic redevelopment or a new-build in the form of a loft,' says Martin Ostermann, founder of Berlin-based architects magma, which converted a former warehouse in east London into a loft (see page 158). Giuseppe Lignano, founding partner of New York architects LOT/EK, which became well known in the 1990s for transforming unusual or difficult sites

into lofts, agrees: 'There's more of a "new" loft movement now rather than a warehouse conversion movement, even though that is still very much going on. All of it has become completely commercial and bourgeois.'

Of course, there have always been other options for urban living and smart developers eager to stay ahead of the game started exploiting these. MLC has branched into hotels, new builds and commercial spaces while, as Tom Bloxham of Urban Splash explains: 'Urban Splash built its reputation on rescuing unwanted and unloved Victorian warehouses in Manchester and Liverpool city centres and we are now rediscovering iconic 60s buildings like Park Hill, Sheffield and the Rotunda office tower in Birmingham.'

Characteristically, Bloxham is using trusted designers to carry out conversions that remain sympathetic to the original buildings, while providing homes for what he calls 'design-minded individuals'. And the latter appear to be a growing breed. A recent project, Chimney Pot Park, involved the conversion of 349 terraced houses in Salford. These two-up, two-down cottages, of the type immortalized in the British soap opera *Coronation Street*, are the backbone of many a northern city and icons of the nation's housing. In a clever but simple move, Bloxham switched the living areas around, creating a

THE BUDENBERG OFFICE BUILDING IN
ALTRINCHAM, CHESHIRE, UK, WAS
CONVERTED BY DEVELOPERS URBAN
SPLASH INTO 33 APARTMENTS IN
1995.

THE HISTORIC SILK WAREHOUSE IN
BRADFORD, UK, WAS THE FIRST
BUILDING TO BE DEVELOPED BY URBAN
SPLASH - THE FIRST OF 131
APARTMENTS WENT ON SALE IN 2004
AND FORM PART OF A LARGER PLANNED
DEVELOPMENT CALLED LISTER MILLS.

double-height living room and kitchen and raised garden on the first-floor, with bedrooms and bathrooms on the ground floor. The framework and façades of the houses remain unchanged except for the chimney stacks, which have been reinstated as modern chimneys. The first batch of remodelled terraces went up for sale in spring, 2006, and people queued for days to buy them.

In Berlin, the loft movement has come full circle, with the area of Kreuzberg, where loft conversions started in the 1960s, once again setting the trends. Mitte, Prenzlauberg and other eastern parts of the city have become so urbane and overdeveloped that Kreuzberg, with its cheap rents, good infrastructure and high concentration of small shops and artisans, holds fresh appeal. 'The loft movement is still important but it's not surprising anymore. And people have realized that it can be uncomfortable, that it doesn't necessarily create a homely feeling,' says Franziska Kessler, one half of Zurich-based creative consultancy Kessler + Kessler. 'What's more, people are moving back into old bourgeois apartments in West Berlin again, where rents are cheaper and there's a firmly entrenched lifestyle on the doorstep.' Having overbuilt in the 1990s, to welcome industry and finance that has yet to arrive, Berlin differs from other German cities in that it has no shortage of housing or office space. Buildings in the city centre are being con-

verted into homes, but for various reasons to do with changing patterns of ownership. For example, many small, individually owned hotels from the 1970s and 1980s have been forced out of business by the arrival of the big chains. Bought by developers, these buildings are being turned into serviced apartments, catering to second-home owners and peripatetic employees of large corporations. Changing a building's use in this way allows the cost-cutting of daily services – for example, where once there was room service, there is now a kitchenette, and the foyer, instead of hosting a bar, lobby and restaurant, is home to a concierge and mini coffee bar.

URBAN REGENERATION VIA CONVERSION
What is the next step for cities where the lofts have already been converted? Other buildings, including churches, schools, ex-shops, ex-municipal spaces and even smaller lofts, are sought, not only by individuals but also by city councils. In Switzerland, the municipality of Bern has proposed a radical overhaul of the city's infrastructure in order to breathe life back into its centre. It plans to move the fire brigade, university, army and many offices out to the suburbs, reclaiming their buildings to transform them into apartments. Drab post-World War II housing, which no-one (not even students) wants to live in anymore will be converted into bigger family apartments and office towers will provide smart homes with great views for a new flush of residents. In Winterthur, near Zürich, a similarly regenerative project involved the conversion of a former train factory into apartments and ateliers, providing the blueprint for the Bern idea.

A TYPICAL LOFT BUILDING IN BERLIN'S KREUZBERG DISTRICT. IN THE 1970s MANY OF THESE ABANDONED BUILDINGS WERE OCCUPIED BY ARTISTS, POLITICAL ACTIVISTS AND OTHERS, OFTEN AS A PROTEST AGAINST THEIR DEMOLITION.

THIS BUILDING FORMS PART OF THE CITY OF BERN'S ONGOING PROJECT TO CREATE HOUSING FROM FORMER OFFICE SPACE.

A VIEW OF HAMBURG'S HAFENCITY REGENERATION PROJECT: NEW BUILDINGS AT SANDTORKAI WITH THE HISTORIC RED BRICK WAREHOUSES OF THE SPEICHERSTADT DISTRICT IN THE BACKGROUND.

Across Europe, city centres have been revitalized through architecture. From Bradford to Barcelona, the conversion of docks, warehouses, storage facilities and factories into homes, shops and service industries has drawn people back to the heart of the city. In cities with historic, heavyweight architecture, there is no choice but to renovate rather than demolish.

Carsten Venus, director of the Hamburg-based practice blauraum, which transformed a 1970s car park on

COMPUTER RENDERING OF AN APARTMENT UNDER THE EAVES OF THE HISTORIC MIDLAND GRAND HOTEL AT ST PANCRAS STATION, LONDON, CURRENTLY BEING DEVELOPED BY MANHATTAN LOFT CORPORATION.

the city's Bogenallee into apartments (see page 122), says: 'Converting old buildings into homes is a growing trend in Germany. Even if the number of households is not increasing, people want more individual living space. Hamburg is going through a massive real estate boom but it is still losing people to the suburbs.' Creating suburbs is costly and vertical living is a cheaper option that makes fewer demands on the infrastructure and precious countryside. 'There are many buildings from the 1960s and 1970s that are ripe for conversion. They have poor technical facilities and their façades are in bad condition, so they need investment anyway. But they have a good concrete skeleton which makes conversion an economically viable option,' adds Venus.

In Hamburg, as well, a project is underway to transform the dock area, Barcelona-style, and increase the size of the city centre by 40 per cent. HafenCity is a 1.6 million square metre (more than 17 million square foot) space that will link the Alster Lake and Elbe River. It will consist of shops, businesses, cultural and leisure facilities, as well as making space for 12,000 new residents in 5,500 apartments. At its heart will be the Uberseequartier, running along the banks of the Elbe. With its maritime centre, cruise terminal and shopping streets, the focus is on leisure, but the area will also provide space into which Hamburg's burgeoning city centre can expand. The red brick warehouses of the Speicherstadt area will be converted into housing and incorporated into HafenCity, which is set for completion in 2009.

In London, another of Europe's largest urban regeneration projects is in progress. The redevelopment of King's Cross encapsulates a 750,000 square metre (more than 8 million square foot) site and aims to transform an urban wasteland and the deprived streets around King's Cross station into a new transport hub and residential neighbourhood. Two train termini, St Pancras International and King's Cross Main Line, will improve train links across the UK and, via a Channel Tunnel rail link, cut journey times to Brussels and Paris to little more than two hours. Due to be fully completed in 2020, this £2 billion project is on course to create 250 businesses, 25,000 jobs, 20 new streets and 10 new major public spaces. In the process, 20 historic buildings will be transformed into housing, among which is the glorious Gothic Revival Midland Grand Hotel. Being developed by the Manhattan Loft Company, it will open in 2010 as a five-star hotel with 68 serviced apartments, most of which have already been sold off-plan.

The ambitious King's Cross regeneration project also includes the area's iconic gasometers, three of

ARGENT DEVELOPERS' PLANS FOR THE KINGS CROSS CENTRAL SITE IN LONDON INCLUDE THE CONVERSION OF HISTORIC BUILDINGS, INCLUDING GASOMETERS (TOP) AND THE GRANARY BUILDING (BELOW). THE MASTERPLAN HAS PROVISION FOR 1,946 NEW HOMES.

which are coming out of storage. Plans for their use have not been finalized but the developers, Argent, intend to convert the gasometers, which are linked, into a mixed development that will include homes, public spaces on the ground floors and, for one, a restaurant on the top level. The gasometer already on site will be relocated next to the triumvirate and enclose a park with play facilities and open spaces. In Vienna, the development of disused gasometers has already been successfully tried and tested (see page 174).

In the 1990s, the city council of Melbourne, Australia, embarked upon Postcode 3000, a massive initiative to rejuvenate the city. It converted old building stock into housing and mixed-use developments, attracting a new generation of urbanites who invested in the local cafés and service industries, and resuscitated a city that was once dead after dark. Melbourne now holds the architectural high ground among Australia's cities. The General Post Office has been converted into shops and restaurants, the National Australia Bank into up-market shops, and the Queen Victoria, an old hospital site, has been redeveloped to create new apartments, shops and restaurants.

Flinders Lane, the location of the loft apartment by rice & skinner (see page 142), is a separate story. The centre of the rag trade from the 1950s to the 1970s, it languished for a couple of decades before being transformed into Melbourne's version of London's Soho. Known as 'The Quarter', it buzzes with galleries, studios and cafés, and has the necessary mix of converted warehouse spaces, renovated heritage buildings and new statement architecture.

For every success, such as Postcode 3000, there is redevelopment that fails to be more than a pastiche. According to Sioux Clark, one half of Multiplicity Architects, based in Brunswick, Victoria, who worked on the conversion of the church in Glenlyon (see page 50), the development of the Melbourne docklands was an exercise in what not to do. 'It paid little attention to the notion of "place" and the way in which history and meaning are layered over time,' she says, adding, 'What happens in Melbourne is atypical of what is going on elsewhere in the country. Suburban ideals are still treasured by most Australians. But there is now some fabricated perversion of the dream reproducing itself across our land. In Victoria, there's a new level of madness whereby outer suburban centres try to emulate urban living environments.' In this new form of housing, warehouse-style living is replicated in crude shells that have never seen industry or commerce, and have no justification for their existence. As a result they exhibit only a superficial understanding of what makes genuine buildings of this nature good to inhabit.

Until a few years ago Los Angeles was another city with a dead-by-night centre, carelessly created sprawling suburbs and an abundance of land around its perimeter. Like some Australian cities, it has undergone - and is still undergoing - a major transformation through adaptive re-use projects. Currently, between 30 to 40 per cent of all building projects in downtown Los Angeles are conversions, while throughout the rest of the city new construction is the norm. The Los Angeles Downtown Center Business Improvement District (LADCBID), a coalition of 480 property owners, has been helping to regenerate the 65-block central business district and transform it into a popular place to live, work and play since 1998. Among their projects is the 'artists' district', an area filled with industrial and former railroad buildings that were colonized by the Los Angeles art community in the 1990s and have

IN THE WAKE OF THE REGENERATION OF THE LOS ANGELES ARTISTS' DISTRICT, THE SOUTHERN CALIFORNIA INSTITUTE OF ARCHITECTURE (SCI-ARC) HAS MOVED INTO THIS CONVERTED HISTORIC RAILROAD BUILDING.

AT HANDELSHOF ST GEORG, BLAURAUM ARCHITECTS HAVE SYMPATHETICALLY CONVERTED HAMBURG'S HISTORIC 1914 TRADE EXCHANGE BUILDING BY FRITZ HÖGER INTO APARTMENTS.

URBAN SPLASH IS CURRENTLY DEVELOPING THE 1960s ROTUNDA OFFICE BLOCK IN BIRMINGHAM, WITH PLANS FOR 232 APARTMENTS.

put Los Angeles on the map as a global art hub. By the millennium, the popularity of the neighbourhood started attracting wealthier residents in search of the 'artist lifestyle' and the district acquired a well-respected cultural tenant when the Southern California Institute of Architecture (SCI-ARC) moved in, occupying a converted historic railroad building.

THE OFFICE TRANSFORMED

Germany appears to be spearheading a new trend for the conversion of offices into apartments. Martin Ostermann of magma architecture explains: 'Offices take up too much space in the city centre, and they have the potential to make ideal housing because they have great views and people love open spaces.' Carsten Venus of blauraum architects, who planned the conversion of Handelshof St Georg – a trade exchange building by Fritz Höger dating from 1914 – into apartments in Hamburg says: 'People want more individual living space, bigger kitchens, bigger bathrooms and this is often only possible within the structure of office buildings.' He predicts that, from now on, the conversion of offices into homes will account for around a quarter of all city centre regeneration in Hamburg. New builds, extensions and new buildings on revised sites will make up the remainder.

In Birmingham, UK, the landmark Rotunda building, a 1960s office tower block that sits in the heart of the city centre (known as the Bullring), dominating the skyline, is being converted by Urban Splash into 232 apartments designed by Glenn Howells Architects. Due for completion in 2008, all of the apartments had been sold by early 2006. Says Bloxham: 'In most large British cities now, the Victorian building stock has been recycled and used up, but there are still plenty of 1960s office blocks and housing available for conversion. But in large towns, places like Wigan and Oldham, there are still many opportunities to be had with old buildings. Having re-introduced the idea of "city living" to people, it's time to revisit the idea of "town centre living".'

LIVING OVER THE SHOPS

As shopping patterns have changed, and malls and out-of-town centres have taken over from small individually owned shops, retail space holds great potential for conversion. Often the upper floors of buildings used for retail purposes have been neglected in favour of the shop floor, creating scope for redevelopment, but LOTS (the acronym coined by the British government to describe 'living over the shop') throws up practical challenges. It is difficult to add pedestrian axes, entrances and exits to retail spaces, and inserting a domestic solution behind retail frontage can be challenging. Due to the exorbitant rates landlords in the UK can charge for such buildings, few are sold. As a result, the UK lags behind other European cities in the conversion of LOTS properties.

In Vienna, architects must nearly always work with existing buildings. The Austro-Hungarian Empire located industry and its vast, now disused buildings in other cities, leaving Vienna a hub of historical architecture. Extension and conversion is encouraged over demolition, and the trend has been to create roof terraces above existing apartment blocks. Over the past five years, however, many of the city centre shops, housed in nineteenth-century buildings, have closed down, forced out of business by malls. Inexpensive, they typically have raised ground levels, high ceilings and big rooms. They are being converted by a new generation of artists, architects and gallery owners into homes and offices. As a result, the spirit of these old neighbourhoods is changing from commerce to culture. One such example can be seen in the apartment designed by Anna Popelka and Georg Poduschka on Schadekgasse (see page 88).

SUBURBAN SPRAWL

Where land is in abundance, is it more cost effective to tap into the existing infrastructure by converting old buildings or to build from scratch? House building is a famously profligate consumer of natural energy and resources – the apex of which, in terms of wastefulness due to disposability, is the creation of suburbs. Yet building around the edges of towns and cities in less built-up areas often appears to be a cheaper and more desirable alternative to vertical living. As Rob Paulus, the architect who designed the conversion of a former ice factory in Tucson, Arizona (see page 132) explains: 'In Arizona, most Americans are still very tied to the "American Dream" of owning their own home with a yard. Only a handful of people understand the social and environmental benefits of living in a denser community. And land is still fairly plentiful here. Suburban development in

western America has, by and large, a much lower initial cost than tapping into existing infrastructure. This typically means fewer permitting costs and quicker timetables since there are fewer people around to ask for permission to build.' However, with this outlook comes suburban sprawl on an unprecedented level. In her book *A Field Guide to Sprawl* (2004, Norton & Company) Dolores Hayden traces sprawl in rural America. She defines it as 'unregulated growth expressed as a careless new use of land and other resources as well as the abandonment of older buildings … visible waste … visible environmental deterioration … seen in the form of decaying older neighbourhoods, abandoned buildings and derelict or declining transit systems.'

In mega-cities, such as Mexico City and São Paulo, suburban sprawl has reached chronic levels, to the point that these cities are becoming uninhabitable. Both cities are held up as sorry examples of how non-existent urban planning has disastrous consequences. With a population of over 20 million, São Paulo is at saturation point. Lifestyles within these cities are usually limited, with people circulating only within their own or a handful of neighbourhoods. Ideas have been mooted for moving people back into the dangerous and decrepit city centre, but this idea still has a long way to go.

In Scandinavia, population density is not an issue and greenfield sites are in abundance but, in the past decade, suburban sprawl has been strictly controlled. Cities such as Copenhagen, Malmö and Århus have been booming, yet suburban development has dwindled in favour of city living. 'Sustainability is a key issue in Denmark and the desire to improve and enhance the quality of industrial areas is high on the agenda,' says Vibeke Grupe Larsen, a Copenhagen-based architect who runs Scaledenmark (www.scaledenmark.dk), an agency offering tours, lectures and workshops in and around the city. Industrial areas of Copenhagen, such as Norrebro and its harbour, have seen the redevelopment of old warehouses, even grain silos.

Dutch practice MVRDV transformed a pair of silos by wrapping the exterior with curvaceous glass-fronted apartments, leaving the interior as a futuristic lobby. 'A conscious effort is being made to re-use brownfield sites and it's difficult to get permission to build in rural areas,' says Larsen. Unlike other cities such as London and New York, where inner city living appeals most to metropolitan, child-free professionals and creative types, in Copenhagen, Århus, Stockholm and Malmö, a broad range of people, including those with young families, is moving back into the city centre, attracted by good infrastructure, schools and facilities. Even with the insatiable demand for new housing in Copenhagen, the city is not spreading outwards. Instead the focus is on the regeneration of areas such as the islands of Amager and Ørestad.

CONVERSIONS IN THE COUNTRYSIDE

As cities grow ever larger and the pressure on personal and communal space increases, the migration of city folk keen to beat a weekend - or permanent - retreat has grown. According to the Centre for Future Studies, there are currently around 328,000 second-home owners in Britain and the number has risen by 15 per cent in two years. If present trends continue, the number of second homes in Britain could hit 700,000 by 2016. This pattern of migration is similar in other European countries and its impact on rural areas is huge, and has both positive and negative consequences.

Five years ago escape to the countryside would not have been complete without Aga stoves, leaded windows, wellington boots and poor central heating. Today, the rural aesthetic has changed significantly and barns, stables, bothies (a type of rural shelter for farm workers) and chapels are being fitted out with stainless-steel kitchens and Philippe Starck bathrooms; sleek Italian furniture and Scandinavian wood now look as at home in the Basque countryside as they do in Barcelona, and village food chain stores are being replaced with corner shops, organic butchers and bakeries - all of which bring a gentrified feel to the average sleepy hamlet.

London architect Anthony Hudson and his wife Jenny Dale convert Quaker barns in Norfolk into modern holiday retreats with straw bale walls, concrete floors, stainless-steel kitchens and open-plan living areas. By bringing a lightness to the interiors, avoiding the heavy timber and dark beams normally associated with barns, they create spaces on a par with any urban loft - only with wonderful views and green space as well. Urban weekenders may bring an irritatingly affluent attitude to rural regions, but they also invest heavily in country pastimes, pursuits and infrastructures.

'British villages will stand still completely if we're not careful,' reckons London architect Laurie Chetwood, whose madcap Butterfly House is born of a plain 1930s house in Godalming, Surrey, in the UK. He adds: 'Architecturally, they have not moved beyond the 1930s. But things are changing. We are seeing more steel and glass being used in the coun-

tryside and this can only be a good thing.' Designed to be like a caterpillar, chrysalis and butterfly all in one, the Butterfly House is a steel and glass structure with rope ladders as staircases, furniture hanging from the ceiling, a jungle garden with triffid-like planting and a roof formed from wisteria.

However, mass migration of affluent urbanites heading to the best beauty spots of any given country has pushed up house prices, making it impossible for local communities to buy properties and creating a housing shortage. The Centre for Future Studies predicts that there could be as many as 405,000 second-home owners in the UK by 2015, an increase of 24 per cent in ten years. Without a dramatic rise in the rate of building new homes, the UK is likely to suffer a shortfall of more than a million homes by 2022. The part-time nature of these 'live-in-the-city-with-one-foot-in-the-country' dwellers means that rural places turn into ghost towns during the week and the winter months, and are bursting with people in the summer. In the UK, the government is considering the introduction of an extra tax on second properties, and is urging councils in regions popular with second-home owners to purchase properties at market value as soon as they go up for sale and convert them into social housing.

In Spain, despite depopulation of villages and an abundance of second-home owners, the government is eager to attract foreign buyers to boost tourism, one of its biggest sources of revenue. Tax breaks are offered and there's no shortage of building types ripe for conversion. These range from *hórreos* (the elevated cereal storage barns made out wood or stone that are typical of Asturias and Galicia) and the stone mills of the Balearic islands and Castilla, to the abandoned wineries that exist all over the country. In particular, the small villages of the Basque country, a region once characterized by industry, have seen their industrial buildings transformed into houses.

As second-home owners continue to contribute to the problem of fluctuating rural populations and countryside sprawl, perhaps there is a lesson to be learned from Denmark. Danish planning, in rural areas particularly, is dominated by the idea of sustainability. 'A major political issue is how to emphasize villages and towns, so that they have their own recognizable borders, rather than just being non-specific areas,' says Vibeke Grupe Larsen. The number of municipalities is being cut from 179 to 64 and a stricter planning agenda is being imposed, with a focus on the preservation of cultural heritage, which will create specific 'zones' within rural regions. It must be noted that Denmark's approach is not a one-size-fits-all solution; the population of Denmark is 5.5 million people, compared with 40 million in Spain and 60 million in Britain, and the small size of the country means that all areas are easily accessible, thus stemming the trend for urban exodus and rural depopulation. In Norway, while abandoned barns are being bought for housing purposes (see Håbakka Barn, page 40), domestic conversions are running parallel to a series of healthy government initiatives aimed at keeping rural communities alive and preserving heritage. Abandoned buildings are converted into 'open farms', which sell local organic produce and offer educational programs aimed at schoolchildren and visitors.

RADICAL CONVERSIONS
Case studies suggest that New York is more evolved than any other city in the world in maximizing the use of land, working with cramped and awkward sites and recycling old buildings. LOT/EK, which has been involved in the loft movement over the past decade, is one of New York's most radical architectural practices. Founding partner Giuseppe Lignano has always adhered to the ethos that 'The most important factor to consider when recycling buildings into homes is not to destroy the original character and fundamental qualities of the building by trying to make it "cute" or "domesticated".' To that end,

LAURIE CHETWOOD'S BUTTERFLY HOUSE, GODALMING, UK. THE ARCHITECT USED STEEL AND GLASS TO CONVERT A PLAIN 1930s HOUSE INTO A WINGED SPECTACLE.

LOT/EK'S GUZMAN PENTHOUSE IN NEW YORK WAS FORMED FROM TWO SHIPPING CONTAINERS.

IN THE MORTON DUPLEX, LOT/EK
CONVERTED A FLOOR OF A PARKING
GARAGE INTO AN EDGY SPACE WHERE
DISUSED PETROL TANKS SERVE AS
SLEEPING PODS.

WITH SPACE IN CENTRAL BARCELONA
AT A PREMIUM, PATRICIA MENESES
AND IVÁN JUÁREZ ARE CONVERTING AN
OLD WATER TANK ATOP A HISTORIC
BUILDING INTO AN APARTMENT.

LOT/EK's loft conversions are an amalgamation of low and high technologies, recycled industrial elements and exposed existing frameworks. The Guzman Penthouse (1996), for example, consists of two shipping containers, one on top of the other, sited in a tiny mechanical space in the shadow of the Empire State building. In the Morton Duplex (1999), a

BRUCE CAMPBELL'S PLANS FOR
CONVERTING A BOEING 727 INTO A
FAMILY HOME ARE BOTH PERSONAL AND
RADICAL.

petrol tanker is turned into two sleeping pods in a loft developed on the fourth floor of a parking garage. More urban grunge than urban glamour, the LOT/EK lofts retain the early anarchic feel of 1960s lofts; recycled refrigerators are used as storage for TVs and hi-fis, newspaper delivery boxes frame windows and domestic appliances are inserted into stainless steel container walls. Other concepts include using a steel water tank as a shell for an indoor skateboard park and an 18 metre (60 foot) long cut-out of a Boeing 727 as a student facility for the University of Washington, Seattle.

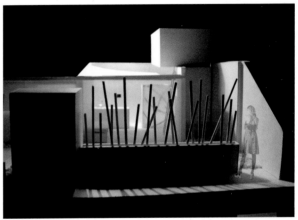

Frequently, conversions are experimental projects that allow a die-hard obsessional to unleash the mad professor within. Bruce Campbell is a self-confessed 'middle-aged technology nerd' who bought a Boeing 727 for $100,000 and has spent the best part of a decade converting it into a family home. It sits on platforms in the middle of a wood in Hillsboro, Oregon, and is something of a local tourist attraction. For Campbell, it was all about having a great toy: 'Trick doors, trick floors. Hatches here, latches there, clever gadgets everywhere. Cool interior lights, awesome exterior lights, titanium ducts, *Star Trek* movies, a *Star Trek*-like setting.' The cabin and cockpit provide 325 square metres (3,500 square feet) of space and Campbell has spent a further $100,000 linking two large cargo holds and bays below the cabin into children's spaces. With a website dedicated to it, the Boeing project is still a work in progress.

Barcelona-based architects Patricia Meneses and Iván Juárez of ex.studio are transforming an old water tank on top of a historic building in the old district of Barcelona into an apartment. A trip to the Texolo waterfall in Veracruz, Mexico, last year also resulted in a concept to transform an old railway bridge into a living area. Located above a gorge in the middle of the jungle, the bridge fell into disrepair when an alternative was built further

downstream. To make the most of the spectacular views, the bridge was wrapped in glass that changes transparency throughout the day. The furnished interior incorporates a long, luminous bathroom block. This suspended living space demonstrates the duo's quest to expose 'new places for living'.

MILITARY MANOEUVRES

In large supply in every country, military buildings are often ripe for recycling where they have become redundant. Throughout the Mediterranean, military buildings that were used to keep control of the busy, political sea, have been converted into leisure resorts and holiday homes. In the United States during the late 1950s and early 1960s, when the Cold War was escalating, the government built 12 Atlas-F underground missile silos, complete with their own hangars and runways, for $18 million apiece. Today, most of these silos lie abandoned and filled with water, monuments to a bygone era of American history. However, one, in the Adirondack State Park in New York State, has been transformed into a 31-hectare (78-acre) luxury retreat by Bruce Francisco and his cousin Gregory Gibbons, a pair of entrepreneurs who bought the land for $100,000. Above ground, they built an unassuming house with a living room and a wrap-around porch. The hub of the house - kitchen, bedrooms and bathrooms - is below ground in what was once the launch control centre. In addition to the living area there are another 4,267 square metres (46,000 square feet) of empty

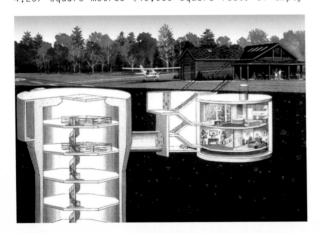

space where the giant Atlas missiles were once stored. Stretching to 55 metres (180 feet) deep, it is hard to imagine how even the most avid art or wine collector would fill it, which might explain why it is still for sale (www.silohome.com).

While military buildings often have a strong structure and prime location, political and social factors can prevent them from being recycled. In Northern Ireland, the recent but tentative peace agreement is leading to the abandonment of many military buildings and Brutalist, concrete police stations across Ulster. Belfast-based artist Rita Duffy has spent the last few years painting and documenting the 12 military watch towers placed along the South Armagh border. Erected by the British in the 1960s, these concrete towers have armour-plated living quarters and underground areas, and command some of the best hillside views in the region. It is easy to see the potential for transforming them into homes in the same way that the fortress-like nineteenth-century Martello Towers, which dot the coastline of mainland Britain, were converted. Yet political factors stand in the way and are leading instead to their demolition. Seen by too many locals as symbols of British oppression, the Ministry of Defence is ripping out the high-tech surveillance equipment within and razing the watch towers to the ground. Duffy, who has documented their demise, was one of a small group who campaigned for their preservation. She is part of a team building a new watch tower, a commemorative landmark building, which will stand on the site of the old.

HOW EASY IS IT TO CONVERT A BUILDING?

The majority of conversions in this book are high-spec individual dwellings, transformed by architects and interior architects running small or medium-sized offices. All demonstrate that it is possible to upgrade and recycle many building types, from schools, churches and warehouses to boats, planes and water towers. However, it can be hard to get permission to do so. In Finland it is extremely difficult, particularly for those wanting to turn a building into a residential space. In the UK too, current planning and building regulations and funding criteria, especially mortgage lending requirements, are so firmly rooted in the measurement of existing products that they stymie innovation. Any architect will say that planning ought to be measured in terms of the physical and cultural ability of a local infrastructure to support density and diversity. Planning departments ought to recognize that the relationship between the two evolves constantly as new lifestyle trends and working patterns inform ideas about the way we live.

With the lack of space in Europe, the architect's

EVER ON THE LOOKOUT FOR UNUSUAL PLACES TO PUT HOMES, MENESES AND JUÁREZ CAME UP WITH THE IDEA OF CONVERTING AN ABANDONED RAILWAY BRIDGE IN THE MEXICAN JUNGLE INTO A LIVING SPACE.

ENTREPRENEURS BRUCE FRANCISCO AND GREGORY GIBBONS HAVE DESIGNED A LUXURY RETREAT WITH VAST UNDERGROUND SPACES IN AN ABANDONED MISSILE SILO IN UPSTATE NEW YORK.

ARCHITECT FIONA NAYLOR AND
PHOTOGRAPHER PETER MARLOW HAVE
SHOWN WHAT CAN BE DONE WITH
DESERTED MILITARY STRUCTURES IN
THE CONVERSION OF THEIR OWN HOME
FROM A MARTELLO TOWER IN
DUNGENESS, ENGLAND.

qualities become the raw material for recapturing and transforming existing structures into "enchanted material".'

Throughout, this book aims to show that recycling old buildings into homes has many advantages. Not only is there an ethical aspect to reusing old building stock, but it can also be a richly creative process. The architects featured on the following pages have manipulated and recombined the materials and spaces available to them to come up with some extraordinary solutions. Given the number of well-located, empty spaces that exist, even in the most populous countries of Europe, it is shocking that we are still building new housing estates on greenfield sites. It is to be hoped that the innovative approaches to converting old buildings shown in these pages will prove that there are alternatives.

dream of realizing a new build is often rare, and there is no choice but to redefine domestic living space within an existing shell. This is both challenging and restricting. Light conditions are often poor; many industrial buildings are large with dark middle areas and small or non-existent windows, so to introduce light, particularly when the façade cannot be interrupted, is awkward. The Rösler barn in eastern Germany, converted by petersen pörksen architects (see page 44) provides a generous space in which a gestural design could be made, within the limitations of the budget. Where the architect is less free to explore spatial qualities, more attention is paid to surface and finish – for example the Workshop House in Saint-Ouen, Paris, France by Nathalie Wolberg (see page 110). Another challenge lies in finding ways to implement the technical infrastructure in old buildings; insulation between apartments, energy consumption, disabled access and circulation can be difficult to incorporate while staying within the often cripplingly restrictive limits of building regulations. Recycling and reinterpretation are the backbone of the young Norwegian practice Helen & Hard (see B-Camp, page 196), for whom using the found and the invented throws up an opportunity to create what they like to call 'retro-visionary playgrounds'. As partner Reinhard Kropf says: 'Disorder, so-called "waste" and forgotten and unfamiliar ideas disturb our daily routines and provide a free space within which a project can develop.' Often, converting spaces provides architects with the chance to develop a sensibility for the sometimes forgotten qualities of atmospheric complexity, vernacular expression and operational pragmatism. Kropf explains: 'For us, these

1

RURAL

APARTMENT BRANDOLINI
David Leclerc Architecture

CADINE DI SOPRA is a small hamlet situated in the picture postcard landscape of the Italian Dolomites within the northern Italian province of Veneto. At an elevation of 1,210 metres (3,970 feet), it is a few miles from the famous ski resort, Cortina d'Ampezzo, one of Europe's most exclusive mountain locations. This idyllic spot was chosen as a weekend pied-à-terre by a couple with three children because it gave access to the ski slopes and was a manageable drive from their home in Venice.

A barn, or *fienile*, which has recently been converted into apartments, sits at the end of a small stretch of road that continues upwards through mountain pastures. The client purchased the barn's attic space, measuring 90 square metres (968 square feet) and split onto two levels. Its construction is typical of the area. Vertical weathered-larch weather boarding is used for the external cladding and a traditional bell-shaped cut out allows light into the top floors. The client wanted to maintain the light and spatial qualities of the original volume while accommodating three bedrooms and two bathrooms. An ideal solution was for the architect to create boat-like cabins that provide berths for the children. The lowest area of the pitch makes an ideal space for the sleeping berths, providing cosy seclusion. The living room and kitchen are placed on the lower level with the master bedroom and en-suite bathroom leading off the

◄ NESTLING IN THE FOOTHILLS OF THE DOLOMITES, THE BARN FEATURES A SMALL CUT-OUT WINDOW, TYPICAL OF THE REGION. THE FAÇADE OF THE BARN HAS BEEN PRESERVED.

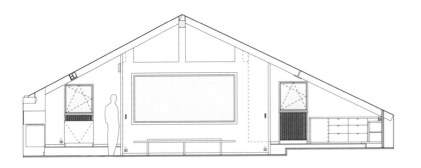
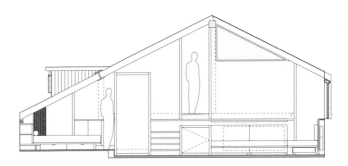

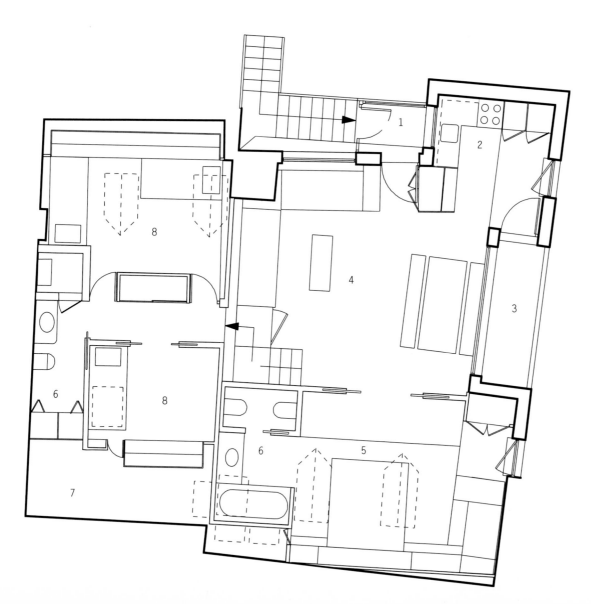

▲ SECTIONS THROUGH THE FRONT AND
BACK OF THE APARTMENT.

◄ PLAN: 1. ENTRANCE, 2. KITCHEN,
3. TERRACE, 4. LIVING AREA,
5. MASTER BEDROOM, 6. BATHROOM,
7. STORAGE, 8. CHILDREN'S BEDROOM

▲ THE LIVING AREA FEATURES
A BUILT-IN SOFA DESIGNED BY
THE ARCHITECT.

▸ THE STUDY CORNER IN THE MAIN
BEDROOM. THE STOOL WAS A GIFT
TO THE OWNERS FROM THE FEDELE
BROTHERS, WHO BUILT MANY OF THE
ADDITIONS TO THE BARN.

◄ LOOKING FROM THE CHILDREN'S BEDROOM ON THE UPPER LEVEL DOWN TOWARDS THE MAIN LIVING SPACE. THE ROOF BEAMS ARE ORIGINAL.

▼ A LARGE PICTURE WINDOW ON THE TERRACE AFFORDS STUNNING VIEWS OF THE SURROUNDING MOUNTAINS. THE WOODEN TABLES AND CHAIRS WERE DESIGNED BY THE ARCHITECT.

living room. In this way the main living spaces profit from the higher floor-to-ceiling height.

The interior becomes a masterpiece of cabinet making with hidden volumes under the stairs doubling as storage areas. Built-in furniture, such as sofa benches and desks, provides a sense of cohesion between the expressed structure and the interior. Sliding doors maximize an impression of space, without wide door swings.

To maintain the sense of lightness, glazed partitions have been introduced where the walls meet the ceiling at a fixed datum level. These clerestory windows allow the immaculately restored roof structure to be clearly visible and give views through it. Rough-hewn circular timber beams span the apex, providing a counterpoint to the planed larch that has been used throughout. Larch is indigenous to the area. In the architect's words 'the rustic "Cortinese style" has been banned'. Instead smooth, minimal construction enhances the fine grain and warm tones of the material.

WHEATFIELD COURTYARD

David McDowell

Malahide

Ireland

◂ A DOUBLE-HEIGHT CEDAR-CLAD BOX
IS THE NODAL POINT OF THE
CONVERSION AND IS THE PLACE AT
WHICH THE TWO BUILDINGS MEET.
IT CONTAINS THE LIVING ROOM AND
MASTER BEDROOM ABOVE.

▸ THE STABLE BLOCK IS AT THE
BOTTOM CENTRE OF THE SITE PLAN.

▾ GROUND-FLOOR PLAN OF THE STABLE
BLOCK. THE CONNECTING BOX IS AT
THE BOTTOM LEFT.

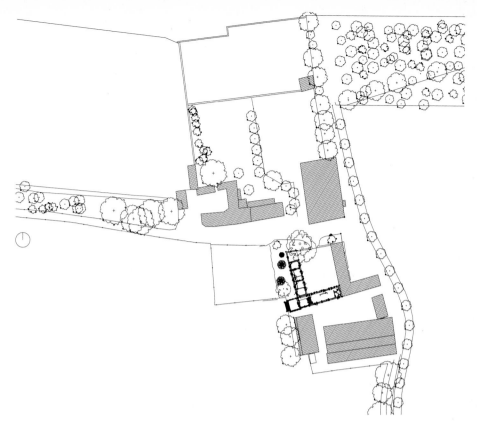

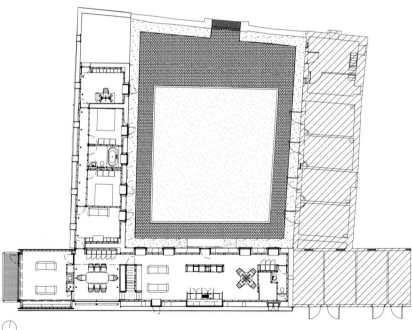

AFTER AN EXTENSIVE PERIOD of working for Britain's top architectural practices, Foster and Partners and Grimshaw and Partners, David McDowell returned home to Ireland to design his own family house in the country-side surrounding Dublin. His response to what is commonly known as 'bungalow blight' - the spread of single-storey houses in rural or greenbelt locations - was to opt to re-use existing building stock. Many randomly grouped farm buildings lay derelict because of the shift away from an agricultural economy.

McDowell purchased a largely derelict stable block, consisting of three buildings of varying heights constructed around a cobbled courtyard with a high stone wall completing the square. He decided to maintain the original forms and arrangement of the stone courtyard buildings while renovating them into a single dwelling unit. The two converted buildings run perpendicular to each other, touching at one corner. At this junction an old building was taken down and a steel frame box inserted, clad in western red cedar timber. The opaque glazed structure acts not only as a connector but also as a light well, allowing light to flood into the interior. The living room and master bedroom are placed within this structure and, in contrast to the inward orientation towards the courtyard typical of the renovated areas, the expanse of glass allows views out onto the surrounding landscape.

The interiors of the buildings were modified over

▴ THE FULLY GLAZED WINDOWS AND OAK DECK OF THE MAIN LIVING SPACE PROVIDE SWEEPING VIEWS OVER THE COUNTRYSIDE.

▾ NORTH ELEVATION WITH THE CEDAR-CLAD BOX TO THE RIGHT.

▴ THE GALVANIZED EXPOSED STEELWORK AND THE RED CEDAR LOUVRES CONTRAST WITH THE ORIGINAL BRICK BUILDING.

▸ THE COMPLEX IS MADE UP OF THREE BUILDINGS OF VARYING HEIGHTS, WHICH LOOK ONTO A COBBLED COURTYARD WITH A HIGH STONE WALL ON THE FOURTH SIDE. THE BUILDING ON THE LEFT REMAINS DERELICT.

▾ SECTION THROUGH THE SOUTH BLOCK, WITH THE CONNECTING BOX ON THE LEFT.

the years to meet changes in farming practice so that
the small number of internal walls were of no historical value. They were therefore removed to leave the
building free for replanning. Where possible, an open-
plan layout was introduced so as to avoid the narrow
corridors to which a long, thin building lke this is
prone. The reuse of all the existing openings in the
external walls maintains the original façade composi-
tions. Recreating the simplicity of the vernacular,
the conversion also provides a sense of drama through
the subtle interventions that create double-height
living space and give an alternative view onto the
landscape.

Externally, McDowell decided to maintain the courtyard, using salvaged cobbles to make a perimeter strip
around it and act as a frame. Surface-mounted external
lights highlight the restraint of the contemporary
details and simple geometry of the existing site.

LA CONCHA

MOOArc

Vale, Guernsey

UK

THE CONVERSION OF a derelict fifteenth-century barn into a contemporary home was awarded an RIBA South East regional award and short-listed for the RIBA Stephen Lawrence award in 2004. It was especially commended by the judges for the fact that its innovative design was achieved within the constraints of one of the most rigorously conservative planning environments in the British Isles - the island of Guernsey.

Jamie Falla of MOOArc, the client and the architect, converted the then derelict barn into an economic three-bedroom family house that blended the old with the new. Overall, 89 suppliers of materials contributed to the house, which took a year to convert. Granite - taken from dismantled walls - is used in both extensions to create doorways, and the floor (mainly heated from underneath) is constructed from polished, recycled glass.

The barn formed part of a traditional fifteenth century Guernsey farmhouse complex which, after planning permission was granted for change of use, had been divided into two. It sits on a linear strip measuring 100 metres (328 feet) long and 12 metres (39 feet) wide, running north to south with the main entrance facing south. The design proposal created one sleeping block, separate from the main living area, linked to the barn via a transparent glazed portal, which the architects describe as 'an

▸ THE MAIN BARN AND THE BEDROOM WING ARE CONNECTED BY A LINKING GLASS BOX.

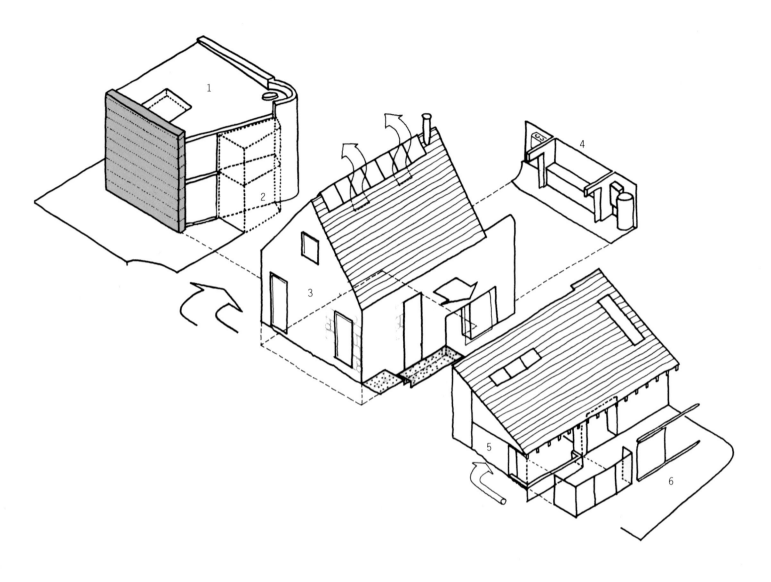

▲ DIAGRAM OF THE FARMHOUSE
COMPLEX. 1. BEDROOM BLOCK,
2. GLAZED LINK, 3. EXISTING
BARN/LIVING AREA, 4. SERVICES,
5. EXISTING LEAN-TO/PLAY, WORK,
GUEST AREA, 6. PUBLIC COURTYARD

◀ SECTION: THE BEDROOM BLOCK IS ON
THE LEFT AND THE LEAN-TO IS ON THE
RIGHT.

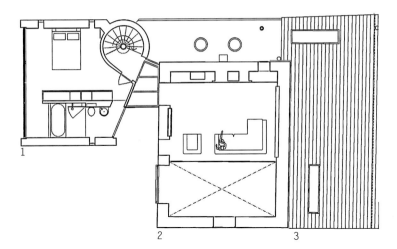

opportunity for the mass of the original barn to breathe'. This modern intervention not only links the two units but allows guests to be observed when entering across the decked courtyard.

To construct the glazed unit, a 50 × 50 millimetre (2 × 2 inch) stainless steel angle frame with two layers of 10 millimetre ($^3_8$ inch) and one layer of 8.8 millimetre ($^1_4$ inch) laminated glass is jointed using laminated silicone. Soft wood lining is used to renovate the underside of the pitched roof within the retained structure of the barn, bringing warmth to the single volume space and acting as an acoustic deadener. This space can be fully opened out to the garden.

For a gradual delineation between public and private areas, the design creates three distinct elements. The first block under the existing lean-to accommodates the studio and guestroom. Being double height, the central space is the core for family activities, housing the kitchen and dining room. A two-storey rear wing with a large glazed wall accommodates the three bedrooms, which face north onto the garden. Above the kitchen/dining room a mezzanine level provides a retreat within which it is still possible to feel part of the activities. At the front of the house, the living/play area opens out onto the south-facing courtyard, which forms the main entrance.

▲ FIRST-FLOOR PLAN. 1. BEDROOM BLOCK. 2. MAIN BARN. 3. LEAN-TO

◄ SKYLIGHTS AND PICTURE WINDOWS ALLOW LIGHT TO FLOOD INTO THE TWO-STOREY BEDROOM EXTENSION (AT LEFT). THE BARN (AT THE RIGHT OF THE PHOTOGRAPH) IS THE MAIN HUB OF THE HOUSE.

The property successfully combines a modern family living space with a contemporary re-reading of the local building crafts, using traditional materials such as the slate and lime render on the external façades. Granite, indigenous to the island, is also used creatively within the design.

MOOArc, established in 1996 by Jamie Falla, has now expanded its practice from the Guernsey office, opening an office in London to develop a broad range of high-quality residential and commercial projects.

▲ THE LINKING GLASS BOX CORRIDOR AND LARGE SLIDING GLASS DOORS ALLOW AS MUCH LIGHT AS POSSIBLE TO FLOOD THE BARN.

◄ THE DINING ROOM WITH THE MEZZANINE JUST VISIBLE AT TOP RIGHT.

◄ THE KITCHEN WITH THE MEZZANINE ABOVE. ON THE CEILING REDWOOD STRIPS WERE NAILED UP TO COVER THE RAFTERS. AT THE APEX ARE SKYLIGHTS.

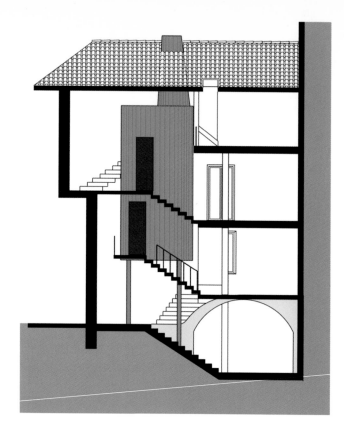

SIMONE CARENA, Stefano Pujatti and Alberto Del Maschio set up Elastico in 1995. Its broad scope includes public buildings from bookstores to cemeteries, as well as private homes. The architects describe their work as 'high altitude experimentation and down to earth developments'. With a sister company, Elastico Design, producing graphics, product design and furniture, the practice's approach stems from a strong multidisciplinary background.

Casa Negro is located in the centre of Cambiano, previously a rural community on the outskirts of Turin that has now become subsumed into the city. The house was once a typical rural barn with pitched roof. Originally its ground floor functioned as a small cow shed, with hay storage above. It overlooks a private courtyard and there is a stable situated at the rear of the plot. Plans are in progress to convert the building, adding an indoor pool with gym and a vast garage space for the family's collection of luxury cars.

With a slim structure, the building has three levels each measuring only 40 square metres (430 square feet). A vaulted cellar provides a storage area for wine and fresh goods. Urban planning restrictions do not permit large volume extensions to the rear of the property so all interventions have been to the interior with the exception of an external staircase.

As the building faces north, the architects decided to open up the rear to let in light. A shift in ground

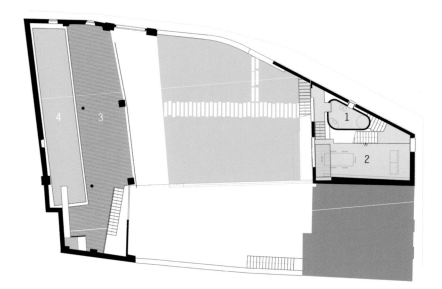

CASA NEGRO

Elastico

Cambiano

Italy

‹ SECTION SHOWING THE DISTINCTIVE CENTRAL ORANGE SILO THAT HOUSES THE SERVICES.

› THE ORIGINAL FAÇADE ALONG THE MAIN ROAD WAS LEFT INTACT, AS STIPULATED BY LOCAL BUILDING GUIDELINES. THE ORANGE SILO CAN JUST BE SEEN THROUGH THE FIRST-FLOOR WINDOW.

⬎ PLAN OF THE HOUSE COMPLEX. 1. ENTRANCE, 2. LIVING AREA, 3. GYMNASIUM, 4. POOL.

◀◀ THE MAIN ENTRANCE FROM THE INNER COURTYARD. THE EXTERNAL STAIRCASE BECOMES A BALCONY THAT LEADS INTO THE KITCHEN AND DINING ROOM.

◀ THE ENTRANCE FROM THE INNER COURTYARD, WITH STAIRS LEADING UP TO THE KITCHEN.

▶ THE MASTER BEDROOM AND BATHROOM ON THE UNDER-ROOF LEVEL. THE BATHROOM FACILITIES IN THE SILO FEATURE SMOOTHLY FLOWING FORMS AND SHINY, ELECTRIC BLUE RESIN SURFACES.

◀◀ THE ENTRANCE LEVEL HAS A CURVED PARQUET FLOOR AND IN-SITU CAST CONCRETE STAIRS. THE REAR WALL RETAINS THE ONLY ORIGINAL BRICKWORK IN THE CONVERSION.

◀ A SHINY, ELECTRIC-BLUE BATHROOM HOUSED INSIDE THE RESIN SILO.

levels meant that the original ground floor was split level. The architects chose to keep the split level and the old structure at the front but to demolish it at the rear. An alien structure – an orange silo – contains the bathrooms. The silo introduces a bold new vocabulary and contrasts strongly with the raw surfaces of unrendered brick and concrete. The architects describe this approach as a form of 'excavation of the original house which is then filled with an orange volume that hosts the programme of new functions'.

Finding the original circulation system in the building chaotic, the architects introduced a clear structure for vertical circulation. Cast in-situ stairs rise from the curved floor plane, covered in a hardwearing industrial parquet flooring. An external staircase wraps around the building and becomes a generous south-facing balcony leading into the kitchen and dining room. A mixture of bare-faced concrete and wood-grain-textured concrete provides a rawness to the structure that harks back to its history as a semi-agrarian dwelling.

HÅBAKKA FARM
3RW arkitekter

BASED IN BERGEN, 3RW has amassed a wide portfolio of work ranging from private houses to a recent commission for a viewing platform overlooking Norway's spectacular Geiranger Fjord.

For Håbakka Farm, the commission was to convert a cluster of farm buildings in a remote area of south-west Norway into a home for a school teacher, his wife and two children. Håbakka Farm is located in the Rosendal region and lies at the end of a track, sandwiched between a fjord and forested mountain.

The 'tun', the Norwegian term given to this type of farm building development, consists of seven buildings that probably date back to the seventeenth century. It would typically have housed generations of the same family or a small community, and has undergone a series of transformations. One of the buildings was relocated from a neighbouring farm 80 years ago and reassembled on a base made of local stone. The base was constructed to allow the building to sit sympathetically in the sloping landscape. Named 'Sara-stova', 'Sara' after the previous inhabitant and 'stova' meaning a wooden log building, the relocated building is approximately 100-150 years old.

The conversion of farm buildings to suit contemporary needs has resulted in a variety of interesting typologies. A common solution, described as the 'long house', extends the typical pitched roofed structure, creating an add-on for extra living space. The farm's

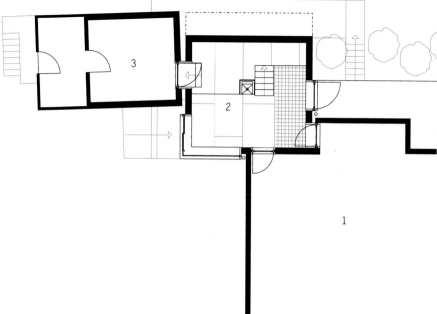

▲ PLAN OF THE FARM COMPLEX.
1. MAIN FARMHOUSE, 2. SPLIT-LEVEL ADDITION WITH LIVING AREA,
3. RESIDENCE FOR OLDEST CHILD

◄ COMPUTER MODEL OF THE COMPLEX. THE EXISTING BUILDINGS WERE KEPT IN THEIR ORIGINAL CONDITION AND THE NEW WOODEN BOX ADDITION WAS BASED ON A TRADITIONAL NORWEGIAN 'LONG HOUSE'.

▶ THE FARM BEFORE CONVERSION. THE WHITE FARM BUILDING TO THE RIGHT OF THE PHOTOGRAPH WAS THE ORIGINAL MAIN LIVING AREA, WHILE THE MIDDLE BUILDING WOULD HAVE BEEN USED TO HOUSE GRANDPARENTS.

▶ THE FARM AFTER CONVERSION, WITH THE GLAZED AND WOOD-CLAD BOX ADDITION LINKING THE TWO ORIGINAL BUILDINGS.

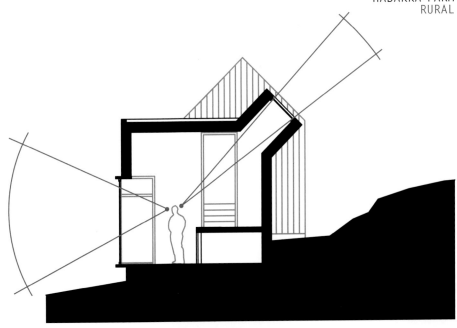

original dwelling, 'Vaningshus', houses the kitchen, bathroom, living room and garden entrance, with two bedrooms on the first floor. To create an additional living area with a sitting room, bedroom for a teenage daughter and climatized shed, the client wanted to link Vaningshus to Sara-Stova. To accomplish this, 3RW created a large, informal lobby space of 24 square metres (258 square feet), which allows access to the garden at the rear. At the front, an opening constructed of large, glazed panels provides views onto the fjord and makes maximum use of natural daylight.

The space is on two levels to accommodate the gradient of the land. A strip of windows at roof level provides views to the mountain. Additional insulation was used in the north façade to equip it against severe cold. Although the brief specified that the new building act as a link, it was not prescriptive as to how the space would be used. The architects therefore decided on a resilient floor covering of shuttering ply, so that the space could be easily adapted later.

To give the extension a contemporary look, the architects chose not to paint the cladding as is normal practice. Instead, selected boards of corewood were chosen from the resilient local pine. The extension complements the simplicity of the 'tun'. Its distinctive form provides an elegant solution that meets modern-day family requirements while allowing the chronology of the buildings to be appreciated.

FOR DECADES THE BARN by Lake Schaalsee in Mecklenburg was cut off from its idyllic lakeside frontage. The former east-German border ran a few metres in front of the barn and severed it from the lake. Rich in natural landscape features, the area's ornate farmhouses bear witness to the prosperity of earlier generations. Situated within a charming hedgerow landscape, the barn benefits from the remains of woods, bogs and wetlands that were shaped by farmers in the eighteenth century.

A typical agricultural structure, the barn has a course of bricks forming the outer wall. Its roof structure is held up with a carefully engineered system of wooden beams and trusses, restored and left exposed. Almost continuously occupied from its inception in the late-eighteenth century to the present day, the barn has undergone many additions and changes. To convert it for vehicle storage, a corbelled roof structure was built, articulated by the large arched openings on the east façade.

The floor area of the barn totals 400 square metres (4,300 square feet), which was considered by the client to be too large to inhabit and too costly to restore. Instead a plywood box was inserted, containing two floors. The box looks at if it is freestanding but it is supported by the existing walls of the barn, which have been strengthened. On the ground floor there are three large spaces housing the dining room,

▲ THE BARN, A MINIMAL WOODEN CONSTRUCTION ENCLOSED IN BRICKS, WAS UNOCCUPIED SINCE THE 1990S, AND IS NOT TYPICAL OF OTHER DWELLINGS IN TECHIN.

▾ SECTION THROUGH THE BARN. THE MAIN LIVING AREA IS TO THE LEFT, SHADED IN YELLOW.

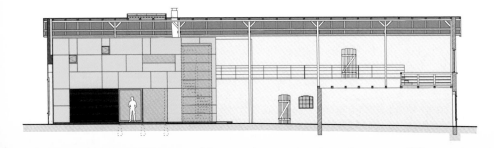

▸ ONLY ABOUT ONE THIRD OF THE BULIDING WAS CONVERTED INTO LIVING SPACE. THE REST IS A FORM OF COVERED 'COURTYARD' AND A PLAY AREA FOR THE CHILDREN. THE EXTERIOR WAS ONLY PARTIALLY RENOVATED.

‹ THE LIVING AREA EXISTS IN A
PLYWOOD BOX INSERTED INTO THE
SPACE. THE METAL CYLINDER,
REMINISCENT OF A GRAIN SILO,
CONTAINS THE STAIRS.

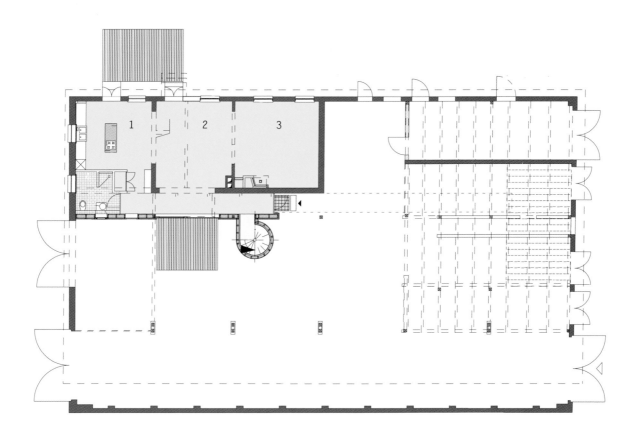

▲GROUND-FLOOR PLAN. 1. KITCHEN,
2. DINING ROOM, 3. LIVING ROOM,
4. BATHROOM

▶THE PLANK BRIDGE, MADE OF STEEL,
LEADS THROUGH THE FIRST FLOOR
SPACE TO THE TERRACE WITH VIEWS
OVER THE LAKE.

kitchen and living room. These are linked to the upper floor by the staircase which, placed in a metal tower, recreates the language of an agricultural grain silo. The original brick floor of the barn has been restored and provides a robust surface for the living area.

The enormity of the barn allowed a layering process of preservation in which some areas are repaired with minimal intervention, but which still succeeds in creating contemporary living spaces. A galvanized steel balcony leads to a mezzanine floor, providing magnificent views over the lake above what was formerly the hayloft. The plywood box marks its outdoor space with a small platform area that looks like it has been peeled off from the structure.

An original solution to restoration is provided by the design concept of inserting a new structure for functional living. The barn becomes an enlarged fore-court where the totality of the space can be enjoyed both as an internal playground for children and as a semi-external protected area for entertaining guests.

▲ THE FIREPLACES WERE MADE OF
RECYCLED BRICKS, WHICH WERE ALSO
USED THROUGHOUT THE FIRST FLOOR
AND IN THE BATHROOM.

▸ THE KITCHEN CONTAINS A CONCRETE
CENTRAL ISLAND, WHILE FITTED
FURNITURE IS MADE OF BIRCH.

◄ THE HALLWAY INCORPORATES BOTH
WOOD PANELLING AND RECYCLED
BRICK.

▾ THE BATHROOM IS SITUATED OFF THE
KITCHEN AND IS FINISHED WITH
DOUGLAS FIR PANELLING.

▲ THE BLUE-STONE CHURCH WAS BUILT
IN THE 1860s WHEN THE TOWN'S
POPULATION WAS SWOLLEN BY THE
GOLDRUSH. ALTHOUGH IT IS A
HERITAGE SITE, THE ARCHITECTS
MANAGED TO REPLACE THE FLOOR AND
ORIGINAL WOODEN DOORS. THIS IMAGE
SHOWS THE CHURCH INTERIOR DURING
THE CONVERSION.

▸ THE CHURCH REMAINS VIRTUALLY
UNCHANGED FROM THE OUTSIDE,
EXCEPT FOR A NEW DOOR. THE 0.7
HECTARE (1¾ ACRE) SITE WAS
COMPLETELY LANDSCAPED AND
INCLUDES A TENNIS COURT AND
SCULPTURES. AN ADDITIONAL BARN
IS ALSO PLANNED.

WHEN ASKED TO PITCH for the conversion of a former church in Glenlyon, Victoria, Multipicity (who were commissioned separately from, but worked in conjunction with, the landscape artist Mel Ogden) put forward an ambitious design proposal. Permitting the existing structure of the blue-stone church and its ecclesiastical features to be read, it also introduced a narrative for contemporary living. The church architecture is very much part of the domestic intervention and at no time does one become subservient to the other. In this way the design is testimony to the historical and social importance of the church within the local community. It was constructed at the time of the gold rush when vast tracts of Victoria settled in what is now rich potato farming land. Such was the status of the church that an invitation to attend its deconsecration was sent out to the local community.

The clients, a professional couple from Melbourne with small children, presented a challenging brief - to maintain the church's celebratory space and historic ambience while providing a warm domestic environment. Insertions were to have a minimal physical impact on the existing building. Internally, the church has uninterrupted sightlines from north to south, allowing the two major stained-glass windows maximum visual impact. The family's private living spaces are confined to two vertical stacks offset from either side wall. The eastern stack has children's

CHURCH CONVERSION
Multiplicity and Mel Ogden

Glenlyon, Victoria
Australia

▴ THE FORMER FRONT ENTRANCE NOW OPENS ONTO THE GARDEN, DOTTED WITH BOULDERS AND STEEL SCULPTURES.

◂ A FORMAL ENTRANCE WAS CREATED, AND HEDGES WERE PLANTED AROUND THE PERIMETER TO SCREEN OFF THE SITE.

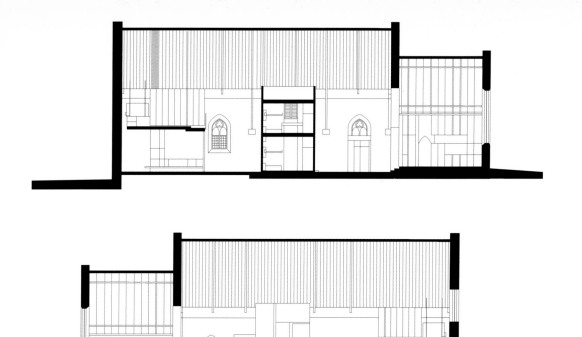

bedrooms with bunk beds at both ground-floor and mezzanine levels, and the western stack provides a laundry and a shower-room at ground-floor level with a bathroom on the mezzanine level. Each stack contains what the architect refers to as 'pods'.

Distinguished by different cladding materials, the pods set up a spatial dialogue between the kitchen and dining area to the south and general living areas to the north. One pod is clad in fluorescent green acrylic to provide a contemporary reading of the muted green of the stained-glass windows. The acrylic's slightly imperfect surface allows it to bend, creating distorted reflections that add to the richness of surfaces in the interior. Picking up on the more traditional language of adornment, the other pod is clad with specially cast plaster tiles; their rich textural appearance acts as a counterpoint to the acrylic folly. A catwalk links the main bedroom and upper-pod levels. As it cantilevers over the living area to provide space for a study, it takes on the form of a church pulpit.

Surrounded on three sides by 22 mature cedars of two species, the site itself is on the corner of the appropriately named Church Street. The longitudinal church building runs north-south, with the original front steps facing north. To the rear, a small sacristy vestibule to one side of the altar leads to a rudimentary timber structure, originally the bell tower.

Behind this, across the rear of the allotment, is a hawthorn-lined carriageway that has been retained for vehicle entry. There are car-parking bays behind the bell tower and a stone path leading down to the bluestone building.

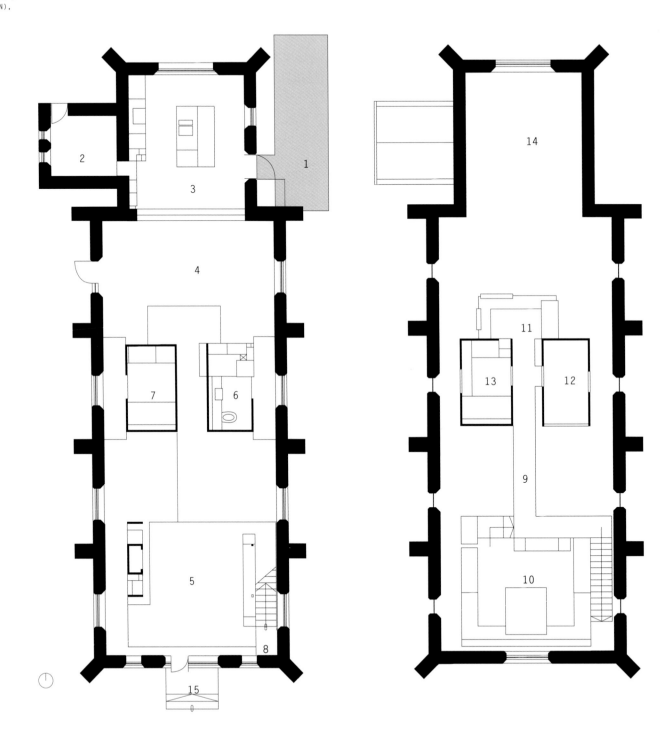

▸FROM LEFT: PLANS OF THE GROUND
FLOOR AND MEZZANINE LEVEL.
1. CLOISTER/ENTRANCE, 2. COAT
ROOM, 3. KITCHEN, 4. DINING AREA,
5. LIVING AREA, 6. BATHROOM,
7. CHILDREN'S BEDROOM,
8. STAIRWAY, 9. BRIDGE,
10. MASTER BEDROOM, 11. STUDY,
12. BATHROOM, 13. BEDROOM,
14. VOID (ABOVE KITCHEN),
15. ORIGINAL ENTRANCE

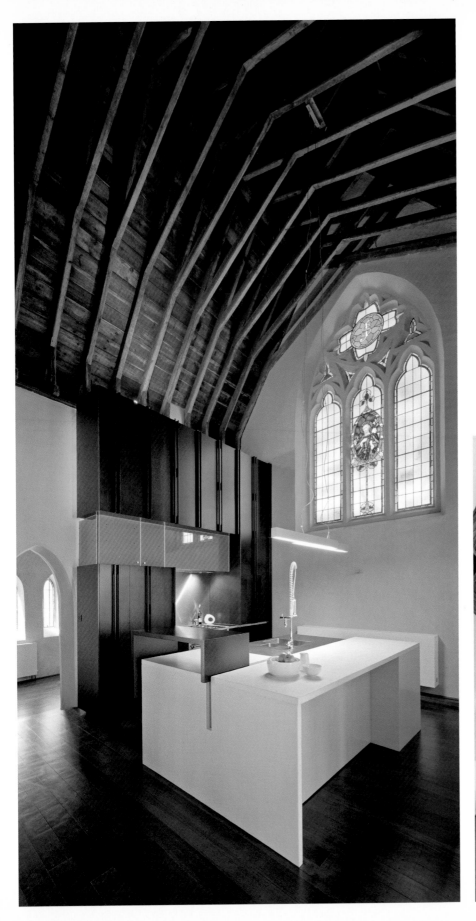

◄ WHERE POSSIBLE, THE OPEN SPACES
OF THE ORIGINAL BUILDING WERE
RESPECTED, WITH A LARGE, DOUBLE-
HEIGHT SPACE AROUND THE KITCHEN
AREA (FORMERLY THE ALTAR).

► THE DINING AREA. VIEWS FROM THE
KITCHEN DOWN THE FORMER NAVE TO
THE REAR OF THE CHURCH WERE
RETAINED ALONG THE NORTH-SOUTH
AXIS.

◂ THE LIVING ROOM AT THE REAR OF THE SPACE. THE GREEN ACRYLIC 'FOLLY' CONTAINS A BEDROOM, WHILE THE WHITE CAST PLASTER TILE BLOCK TO THE LEFT HOUSES A BATHROOM.

▾ STAIRS LEAD FROM THE LIVING ROOM UP TO THE CORRIDOR NEXT TO THE MASTER BEDROOM. THE HEARTH (RIGHT) IS MADE FROM WHITE CONCRETE WITH STEEL PANELLING TO MIMIC THE GARDEN SCULPTURES.

▸ A 'CATWALK' LINKS THE MAIN BEDROOM AND UPPER POD LEVELS, CANTILEVERING BEYOND TO PROVIDE SPACE FOR A PULPIT-LIKE STUDY.

▾ THE MASTER BEDROOM – NOT QUITE THE FULL WIDTH OF THE CHURCH – IS CANTILEVERED SO AS NOT TO TOUCH THE WALLS AND IS ONLY PARTIALLY ENCLOSED BY CABINETS SO THAT THE OWNERS CAN FULLY APPRECIATE THE SPACE.

▲ THE ANCIENT WAREHOUSE BEFORE CONVERSION. THE WIDE SPACE AND THICK WALLS WERE THE BUILDING'S TWO MAIN ATTRACTIONS.

◄ THE WAREHOUSE AFTER CONVERSION. THE ARCHITECTS INSERTED LIVING SPACES USING A SERIES OF 'BOXES' THAT HIGHLIGHT THE SYMMETRY OF THE FAÇADE.

THE LISBON ARCHITECTS Francisco and Manuel Aires Mateus occupy an important place in the current Portuguese architecture scene. Amassing a large number of public and private commissions in their own country, the brothers have won a series of competitions over the last few years. Their work demonstrates an ability to exploit the plastic elements of architecture while drawing on the vernacular style of Portugal's building tradition.

An ancient wine warehouse in a village in the Sétubal region south of Lisbon, with sizeable walls 90 centimetres ($35\frac{1}{2}$ inches) wide, provided an ideal shell for conversion into domestic use. Built originally with low-quality masonry materials such as stone and clay, its roof structure boasts a well-engineered truss system that was restored during the conversion.

Creating a contemporary installation within the existing space has resulted in a dramatic architecture that does not adhere to the conventions of a standard domestic language. Large volumes, conceived as habitable spaces, appear to float above the main space, offsetting the symmetry of the existing architecture.

The architects inserted the stairs within a secondary wall running parallel to the existing perimeter walls, drawing attention to - even exaggerating - their thickness. These perimeter spaces also house the kitchen, social restroom, cloakroom and laundry compartment, thereby entirely freeing up the central

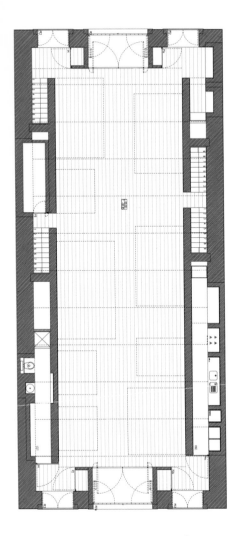

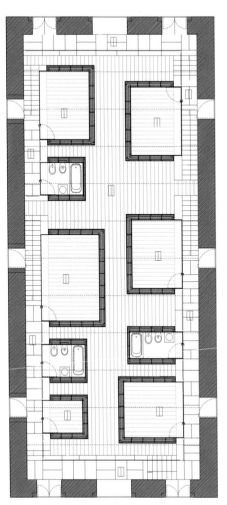

space. The boxes on the upper floor house the bedrooms and bathrooms and are lit with windows cut out of the boxes that line up with the existing windows in the external walls. Explaining the structure of the cantilevered balconies, the architects emphasize their simplicity: 'The structure is much more common than people normally suppose: there's a slab under the boxes' floor that is like a cantilevered "balcony".'

Placing the boxes within the existing space conjures up an effect that recalls the work of Donald Judd, the American minimalist artist and sculptor. Judd's large forms took on a specific language when placed in Marfa, Texas in two converted artillery sheds. As the boxes become inhabited, the occupier is no longer merely a spectator but is interacting with the domestic landscape.

The existing façade has a rational quality and its proportions, ideal for the domestic layout, dictate the programme of the interior.

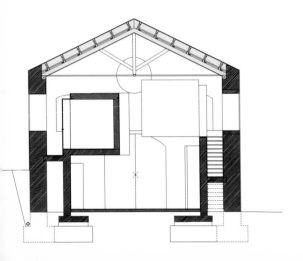

▲ FROM LEFT: GROUND- AND FIRST-FLOOR PLANS. THE SUSPENDED BOXES ON THE UPPER LEVEL HOUSE BEDROOMS AND BATHROOMS AND ARE REACHED BY STAIRS ON EITHER SIDE OF THE BUILDING.

◄ SECTION THROUGH THE HOUSE SHOWING THE SUSPENDED BOXES AND THE ACCESS STAIRCASE TO THE RIGHT.

▲ THE SUSPENDED BOXES SEEN
FROM THE GROUND LEVEL. KITCHEN,
LAUNDRY AND OTHER PRIVATE SPACES
ARE KEPT IN THE PERIMETER SPACES
ON EITHER SIDE OF THE WHITE
INTERIOR WALLS.

◄ THE ARCHITECTS RENOVATED THE
WELL-ENGINEERED ORIGINAL ROOF
TRUSS SYSTEM.

EL CARRIU
aSZ arquts

FOR THIS COMMISSION, the original building was an elegant barn in Bisaurri, situated in the Province of Aragón, Spain. Thought to be 300 years old, the barn appeared in the first recording of Bisaurri's municipal records. It was a typical agricultural building, housing cattle and providing winter storage for hay. In 1934 it was extended to accommodate a shepherd and, in 1964, modernized to house a family, who also maintained the stable.

The client, a journalist who has spent the last 20 years travelling the world working as a foreign correspondent, wanted a retreat to which he could eventually retire. His brief to the architect was fluid, with the only specific requests being for a library in which to display artefacts collected on his travels, and for a private space with independent access. The client had spent his childhood on the land around the property, which belonged to his grandfather. On inheriting the property, he considered two options. The first was to renovate the barn's original structure and restore it in an authentic manner, although it was unclear as to how far back to go in the restoration work. A second option was to add a new structure to the original one. Both the architects and the client wanted to avoid a pastiche of the old, but were also concerned that a contemporary architectural language might be rejected by the local planning authorities.

▲ FRONT AND BACK VIEWS OF THE 300-YEAR-OLD BARN BEFORE CONVERSION.

▶ LAMINATED WOOD, A ZINC ROOF, WHITE BRICK AND THEN CONCRETE SLABS MAKE UP THE NEW STRUCTURE, WHICH SITS ON TOP OF THE 'RUIN' OF RED AND WHITE STONE BELOW.

▲ THE ROOF TILTS TOWARDS THE REAR
OF THE HOUSE AND EXTENDS TO FORM A
PORCH AND COVERED GARAGE. STAIRS
NEXT TO THE GARAGE LEAD UP TO THE
MAIN LEVEL.

▶ PLAN OF THE MAIN LIVING SPACE.
THE FRONT OF THE BARN IS AT THE
BOTTOM AND THE GARAGE AND
ENTRANCE STAIRS ARE AT THE TOP.

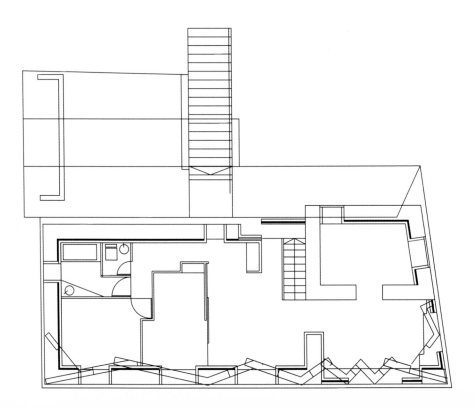

Established in 1990 and based in Barcelona, aSZ architects have undertaken large-scale housing projects, and the practice is considered to be at the forefront of contemporary Spanish architecture. Architects Antonio Sanmartín and Elena Canovas proposed a house that would blend with its environment as well as create a dialogue between the new and the old. The result, El Carriu, was awarded the Premio Garcia Mercadal, a regional architecture prize, for its success in introducing a strong contemporary language that harmonizes with the surrounding landscape and enhances the existing structure.

Within a rural setting, the original barn consisted of a two-storey building set on a sloping site. The architects proposed increasing the façade with an additional two floors as the existing depth was extremely narrow. Antonio Sanmartín talks of the once modest house growing into a piece of architecture with a certain stature. With no specific use prescribed for the lower level, the first and second floors were designed to be used as a holiday house for a family of four, while the upper level contains the library and guest room. Separate access to the library is provided by a single run staircase, which projects from the rear façade.

Local builders commissioned to work on the project, skilled in traditional methods of construction, rose to the challenge of building a new type of structure. The barn's original structure consisted of dry stone walls, which were weak and gave no structural stability. To reinforce the walls so that they would provide a firm foundation for the additional façade, longitudinal supports consisting of concrete blocks were built behind the existing façade. Wooden vertical elements were added to support the window frames and act as bracing elements. Antonio Sanmartín compares the addition of the façade to placing a 'jockey on top of a racing horse', and the result is an elegant structural solution that makes use of the existing building in an ingenious manner.

The decision to facet the new façade was informed by the idea of framing particular views onto the surrounding landscape, while at the same time breaking up the façade so as to reduce the mass of the four-storey building. A zinc roof tops the building, and is pitched at a sharp angle. It covers the main building as well as the once-separate barn structure at the rear of the property, which now houses the garage and porch. This gives the site an overall homogeneity, while folding the roofline at an oblique angle adds structural support to the roof. The architects' decision to introduce the single pitch was a result of the strict planning laws of the Pyrenees area that do not allow the pitch of a roof to be less than 45 degrees.

▸ A SEATING AREA ON THE LOWER LEVEL CONTAINS ARTEFACTS COLLECTED BY THE OWNER. A CANTILEVERED STAIRCASE PROJECTS OUT FROM THE ORIGINAL STONE WALL ON THE LEFT.

COB CORNER

David Sheppard Architects

Ivybridge, Devon

UK

IN RURAL ENGLAND planning policies have recently been introduced to deter some of the less-than-sensitive barn conversions and the consequential damage to wildlife habitats. Therefore, when David Sheppard purchased a Linhay barn in the Erme Valley, Devon, with a view to turning it into a home for himself, he faced the challenge of designing a barn conversion acceptable to local planning authorities. With its open structure housing a cattle shelter with hay loft above, the Linhay barn is a common building type in southwest England and Sheppard set out to exploit the natural features of the vernacular typology.

The original barn was clad in timber with gaps for light and ventilation allowing a clear flow of air for drying animal feed. Each element was constructed with an economy of material and construction detail. The untreated timber and rawness of execution give this type of agricultural building its robust, rustic nature. Sheppard focused on these elements, reintroducing their vocabulary to his conversion so that it retains the fundamental qualities of light penetration, texture and organic colour.

Two-storey barns were traditionally slated, with overhanging eaves to attract nesting birds. As well as reslating the roof of the barn, Sheppard introduced oak timbers in a scissor-truss form to provide additional structural support. A lead gutter was added around the eaves of the barn to collect water, which

► DESPITE ITS DILAPIDATED STATE, THE ORIGINAL BARN HAD TO BE RENOVATED FOLLOWING STRICT LOCAL AUTHORITY GUIDELINES.

◄ THE COMPLETED BARN CONVERSION IS CHARACTERIZED BY ECO-FRIENDLY TOUCHES, SUCH AS EAVES TO ATTRACT NESTING BIRDS AND GUTTERS THAT CARRY RAINWATER TO A POND.

▼ SECTION THROUGH THE BARN WITH THE UPPER MEZZANINE ON THE RIGHT.

▼ GROUND-FLOOR PLAN. 1. KITCHEN, 2. DINING AREA, 3. LIVING AREA, 4. BEDROOMS

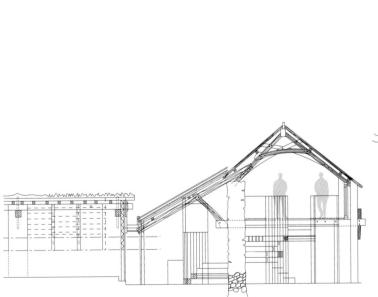

runs into a holding soak away before percolating slowly into reed beds. The water flow terminates at a pond, topped by a natural spring.

Flanking either side of the barn are two single-storey out-house buildings, converted into bedrooms and a studio with connecting corridors. Covered by a sedum roof that changes colour with the seasons, these areas are a refuge for wildlife, attracting butterflies and a variety of insects.

All the barn's glazing is clad with Douglas fir frames, which are unpainted but treated with oil. To reduce the dominance of the glazing, horizontal and vertical slats were introduced to imitate the sense of an empty barn. The slats are made from Keruing hardwood, originally sourced from South East Asia but purchased from a salvage yard. Tongue-and-groove flooring planks were split so that they could be re-used as window louvers. Each slatted frame required minimal cuts to achieve its geometry. Within the studio area, these panels have been used both internally and externally with vertical glass slits allowing shafts of light to penetrate the interior.

◄ OAK TIMBERS, PEGGED AND CUT IN A SCISSOR-TRUSS FORM, ARE A CENTRAL FEATURE OF THE FAÇADE.

▶ THE STUDIO SPACE IN ONE OF THE SEPARATE OUTHOUSE BUILDINGS.

▲ THE LIVING ROOM SITS UNDER THE
OAK TRUSSES IN THE TWO-STOREY
MAIN BARN.

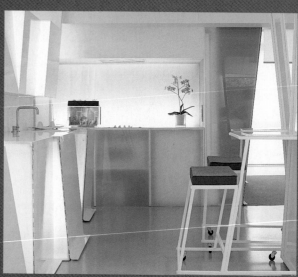

URBAN

CASA CESARI
Massimiliano Vaiani

THE SMALL, HISTORIC TOWN of Campo Bisenzio, north of Florence, is creating its own identity as an attractive alternative to the bustling Tuscan capital.

The architect Massimiliano Vaiani was contacted by a young couple who wanted to live in a large, open-plan living space and were willing to move out of the city to find an alternative to the escalating property prices in Florence as well as a dearth of large industrial spaces available for conversion. The clients bought a warehouse dating back to the sixteenth century, which had in the past supplied the neighbouring country house with farm produce and wine. The scale of the building is domestic in its proportions, and so provided an ideal project on which to apply the clients' requirements: a large, open-plan living and dining space with an office that overlooks the social areas. Planning restrictions dictated that the ground floor had to remain non-residential.

Typically for the area, the building was constructed using a herringbone pattern of bricks and stone with plaster on the interior. At the time of the commission, the building had been abandoned for more than a decade and had fallen into a state of disrepair. Throughout the building's history the space had been adapted for different uses, such as the storage of farm equipment, a cattle shed and grain storage, resulting in an ad-hoc construction of internal walls within the main frame of the building. The building

◄ THE LIVING AREA HAS A GENEROUS
FLOOR-TO-CEILING HEIGHT OF 4.5
METRES (14 FEET 9 INCHES).

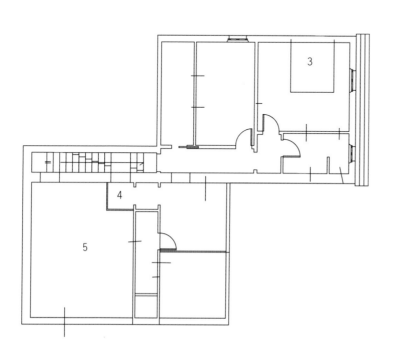

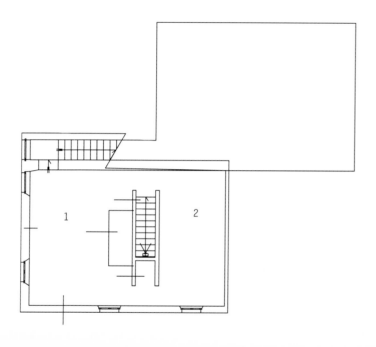

▲ THE HAYLOFT BEFORE CONVERSION.

◄ FROM BOTTOM: PLANS OF THE LOWER AND UPPER LEVELS. 1. LIVING AREA, 2. KITCHEN/DINING, 3. BEDROOM, 4. BALCONY, 5. VOID OVER LIVING AREA

was stripped of these alterations to recover the original volume and the original wooden floorboards on the upper floors, which were, amazingly, largely intact. The architect's aim was to articulate all of the original shell and express the structure, which meant restoring the roof back to its original beam-and-terracotta construction, and stripping off the internal plasterwork. The layout of the conversion has remained very similar to the original, maintaining the principal staircase that runs from the ground floor to the first floor. This staircase has been rebuilt using the local Serena stone. A narrow wooden staircase leads up to the attic floor and the office. Rather than enclose this route the architect has articulated it by inserting a balcony with a toughened glass balustrade, which creates an interesting link between the floors. The space of the balcony carries on to form the mezzanine level of the office. The bedrooms are also on this level under the eaves. The main living space under the single pitch of the building has a generous floor-to-ceiling height of 4.5 metres (14 feet 9 inches). The architects have left an expanse of the existing stone wall - named the 'tapestry' - unrendered to demonstrate the technique of the craftsmanship that went into the construction. Adjacent to this is a large rendered area painted orange and red to indicate the construction of the new walls.

◄ STAIRS OF LOCAL SERENA STONE
LEAD UP TO THE MAIN LIVING SPACE.

▼ SECTION SHOWING THE MEZZANINE
AND BALCONY OVERLOOKING THE
LIVING AREA.

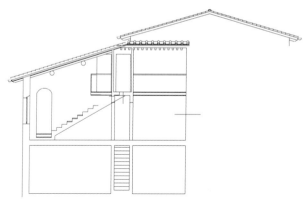

◄ AN OFFICE HAS BEEN TUCKED UNDER
THE SLOPING CEILING ON THE
MEZZANINE LEVEL. THE GLASS
BALUSTRADE ALLOWS LIGHT TO ENTER
THE UPSTAIRS SPACE AS WELL AS
ALLOWING INTERACTION WITH THE
LIVING AREA BELOW.

WESTCLIFF HOUSE

Silvio Rech. Lesley Carstens.

OVER THREE YEARS in the making, the story behind the building of Westcliff House began when the South African architects came across the site during a break from an 18-month work contract in Tanzania. Building a handcrafted African boutique lodge had proved fraught with problems. The husband and wife team recall some of their worst experiences during the construction: 'Against the odds we would be in a remote corner of Africa and get a radio message that a tree had fallen on the house, or that the plaster walls were melting.'

Building up a portfolio of exotic bush camps and luxury resorts over the last five years, the architects have created a distinctive style in response to the regional cultures of their country. They describe their work as a craft-based approach to the design of tourist sites, employing local craftspeople with transferable building skills, and using sustainable materials. Ready to build their own house, they wanted to apply the expertise they had developed. A piece of land nestling the Johannesburg suburb of Westclif, with a forest of overgrown trees and plants and a storm-water river running through it, provided a sense of the wilderness they were seeking. Built by the rand lords, who were mining magnates, the suburb itself is one of the oldest in Johannesburg and part of a strong tradition of early-Johannesburg architecture.

Links with a large pool of African craftspeople and builders from all around the country motivated the architects' decision to design a building that would draw on vernacular skills. The layout was based on that of an African village, which is comprised of a series of huts or rooms that form a compound. This arrangement is then overlaid with a more formal ordering of circulation designed around a central axis. The property housed a small nine metre (29½ foot) rondavel, a round, thatched building that was once used as a German secret society clubhouse. Keeping the rondavel at the heart of the building, the architects decided to raise its thatched roof with an inventive truss work of gum poles to create a generous floor-to-ceiling height. The floor was re-screeded with brown pigment and all the walls were plastered with brown mud from the site. To open up the front of the rondavel, Tanzanian carvers created the frames for large, three metre (10 foot) high windows that are flanked by two sculptural chimneys that rise up as sentinels on each side.

A two metre (6½ foot) high bed in the bedroom overlooks the forest. In front of the bedroom, a deck provides steps down into the garden by means of a rock amphitheatre, giving a magical sense of theatre to the garden. Infill spaces between rooms such as the dining room and bedroom are designed around pure forms - rectangles, circles and semi-circles - with carved niches creating traditional 'poche'. These are filled with sculptures and artefacts. In the bathroom the

◂ THE LIVING ROOM IS THE PRINCIPAL SPACE OF THE ORIGINAL RONDAVEL – A TRADITIONAL ROUND, THATCHED STRUCTURE.

▲ THE ARCHITECTS HAVE FILLED THE
HOUSE WITH FURNITURE THAT THEY
DESIGNED THEMSELVES AND THEN
COMMISSIONED LOCAL CRAFTSMEN
TO PRODUCE.

▶ THE HAND BASINS, WHICH WERE
DESIGNED TO EMULATE UPTURNED
LILIES, SIT ON A PLANK OF LOCALLY
GROWN HARDWOOD.

▲ IN THE KITCHEN THE SEVENTEENTH-
CENTURY STONE WALL IS CONTRASTED
WITH AN ULTRA-MODERN STAINLESS-
STEEL WALL UNIT OPPOSITE.

◄ THE USE OF MIRRORS AND A
COMBINATION OF UP LIGHTERS AND
DOWN LIGHTERS ACCENTUATE THE
BUILDING'S STRUCTURE.

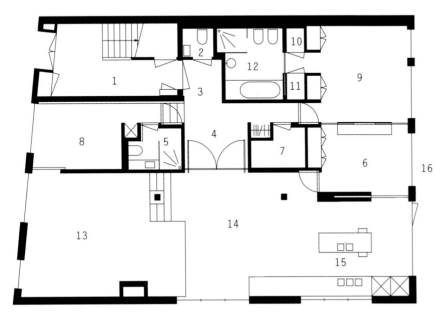

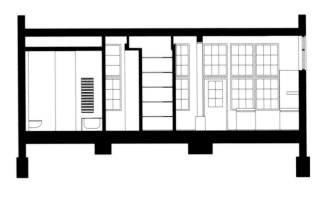

▲ GROUND-FLOOR PLAN. 1. TECHNICAL ROOM. 2. SHARED ENTRANCE. 3. TOILET. 4. HALL. 5. BATHROOM. 6. GUESTROOM. 7. STORAGE. 8. STUDY. 9. BEDROOM. 10. WASHING ROOM. 11. STORAGE. 12. BATHROOM. 13. LIVING AREA. 14. DINING AREA. 15. KITCHEN. 16. GARDEN

▲ SECTION THROUGH THE CENTRE OF THE APARTMENT, WITH THE BATHROOM ON THE LEFT AND THE DINING AND KITCHEN AREAS ON THE RIGHT.

VAN BREESTRAAT IN AMSTERDAM has had an interesting history. Built originally as a horse-tram depot, housing a stable and storage shed for trams, the building was redesigned in 1920 to provide a training school for midwives.

Marc Prosman Architects, a ten-strong practice based in Amsterdam, has completed a number of exquisite and daring renovations, as well as a state-of-the-art equestrian centre in Holland. For Van Breestraat, the client's brief was to convert the building into an apartment that would function both as a private space and a convivial place for entertaining. Designed on one level, the apartment benefits from a deep section with windows on both sides. Due to its industrial history, the building has a generous floor area but the former non-residential conversion ran walls at oblique angles, forming a complicated arrangement of spaces. All the internal partitions were therefore removed and the space overlaid with an orthogonal plan.

With a total floor area of 150 square metres (1,615 square feet), the apartment contains one bedroom and one guest room. On entering from the street the silkscreen glass doors lead straight into the main living space. The original timber buttressed columns with steel brackets align with the new partition walls. Making a grand statement, a bronze sculpted table by the design practice Studio Job is placed

▸ THE WALL DIVIDER IN THE LIVING
AREA FUNCTIONS AS AN ART WALL AND
HOUSES THE FLAT SCREEN TELEVISION
AND AUDIO EQUIPMENT.

▾ THE SAME SANDSTONE FLOORING
HAS BEEN USED THROUGHOUT THE
APARTMENT TO UNIFY THE INTERIOR.

within a minimalist kitchen by the British architect
John Pawson. From this area, the space opens up to the
study with sliding doors that sit flush within the
walls when open. High-quality details that mimic those
of cabinet making form the fixtures and fittings.

Within the apartment a series of sliding and flush
doors permits the total area to be opened up when
accommodating a large number of guests, then easily
closed off to form more intimate and contemplative
spaces. The two bathrooms are clad in white marble,
with travertine flooring reflecting the light.

◂ THE BRITISH MINIMALIST ARCHITECT
JOHN PAWSON WAS BROUGHT IN TO
DESIGN THE SUITABLY MODERNIST
KITCHEN. A 50 MILLIMETRE (1 INCH)
THICK GRANITE WORKTOP SURFACE AND
SINK AREA WERE SPECIFIED.

▸ THE PARTITION WALLS DOUBLE AS
STORAGE OR AS ABSTRACT SCREENS
THAT RELATE TO THE STRUCTURAL
FEATURES OF THE ORIGINAL
BUILDING.

SCHADEKGASSE

PPAG Architekten

Vienna

Austria

THE SCOPE OF PROJECTS carried out by Viennese architects, Anna Popelka and Georg Poduschka, ranges from
an apartment building, a pool, a wind tunnel and an
information centre for contemporary culture. While
each design makes use of different materials and
forms, certain characteristics reoccur - though in
widely varying circumstances.

PPAG Architekten outgrew its original office space,
which had living quarters attached, in a former shop
in one of Vienna's typical nineteenth-century buildings. The office was moved to a different location
and, with the family now grown up, it was decided to
extend the living space to the ground floor. On entering the apartment, its total volume is immediately
evident and it is possible to enjoy a view through the
entire ground floor to a small courtyard that allows
shafts of light to penetrate all areas.

The two floors occupied by the architects have the
advantage of facing south and being orientated towards
Esterhazy Park. Moving the main living space to the
ground floor means that in summer the pavement becomes
a terrace, extending the living area to the exterior.
In the park, there is an original Second World War
Flakturm - a large anti-aircraft gun blockhouse used
by the Luftwaffe to prevent the enemy from flying over
key areas in certain cities. The towers also served as
air-raid shelters for tens of thousands of people and
were used to coordinate air defense.

◀ ▼ LOWER- AND UPPER-LEVEL PLANS
OF THE FINAL LIVING SPACE. 1.
LIVING AREA. 2. KITCHEN. 3.
COURTYARD. 4. BATHROOM. 5. ROOM
ONE. 6. ROOM TWO. 7. GALLERY

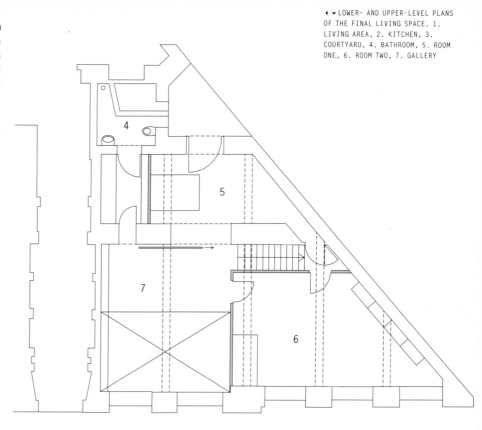

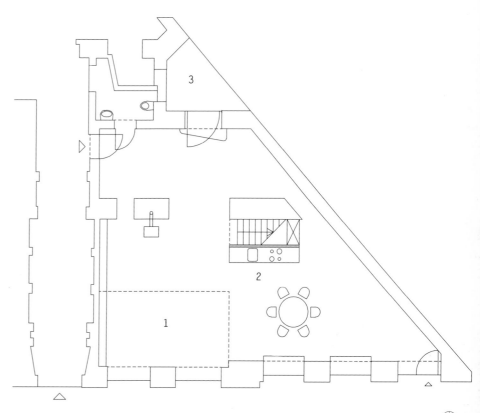

◀ ANNA POPELKA AND GEORG
PODUSCHKA'S ECLECTIC MIX OF
FURNITURE REFLECTS THEIR LONG
RELATIONSHIP WITH THE BUILDING,
WHICH FIRST SERVED SOLELY AS
THEIR OFFICE, THEN AS A LIVE/WORK
SPACE. NOW THE FORMER SHOP
FUNCTIONS AS THEIR HOME.

▸VIEW OF WHAT WAS FORMERLY THE
SHOP AREA.

▸▸THE ARCHITECTS HAVE CHOSEN A
LOFT-TYPE LAYOUT, WHERE THERE ARE
NO DIVISIONS BETWEEN THE LIVING/
DINING/AND COOKING AREAS. PARTLY
DUE TO THE DEEP PLAN OF THE GROUND
FLOOR THIS APPROACH ALLOWS
THE NATURAL LIGHT TO FLOW FROM
THE REAR AND FRONT FAÇADES INTO
THE CENTRE.

▾THE MEZZANINE LEVEL IS
SUPPORTED BY STEEL BEAMS, WHICH
SPAN THE WIDTH OF THE BUILDING.

In 2000, the architects began the work of converting the property. The shop had an extremely generous floor-to-ceiling height of 4.7 metres (15½ feet) and, to take advantage of this volume, an extra floor was introduced of cast concrete 150 millimetres (6 inches) deep. Leaving a void at the street side of the property allows light into the rear. A gallery links the bed-rooms at the first-floor level to the bathroom. The diagonal wall that encloses the site on the street boundary is accentuated with a row of floor-to-ceiling built-in cupboards. Previously used for office equip-ment, these are now part of the kitchen storage system. A sense of openness prevails with bright gloss surfaces and polished concrete floors painted with an epoxy paint normally used for swimming pools.

HOUSE ON THE OUDE DELFT
Christian Müller Architects

Delft
The Netherlands

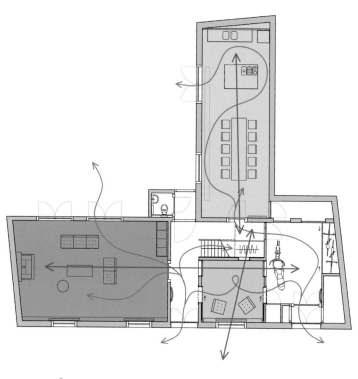

◄ PLAN OF THE RESIDENCE.
SIGHTLINES ARE INDICATED IN RED,
AND CIRCULATION IN BLUE.

▼ THE HOUSE IS SITUATED ON ONE
OF THE CITY'S MOST FAMOUS CANALS,
THE OUDE DELFT, WHERE BUILDINGS
DATE BACK TO THE FOURTEENTH
CENTURY.

CHRISTIAN MÜLLER ARCHITECTS, based in Rotterdam and Zurich, have established a reputation for sensitive but bold modern conversions and renovations, housing projects and an impressive list of competitions wins.

The historic city of Delft is perhaps best known as the birthplace of Vermeer and Delftware blue porcelain. Müller was approached by his client to convert a house on one of the most historic canals in Delft, the Oude Delft. The client was adamant that the house would have a contemporary atmosphere and his brief to the architect was to provide a space that would enable him 'to celebrate contemporary lifestyle in a spacious historic setting'. The house, which dates back some 300 years, has a total floor area of 320 square metres (3,400 square feet) and a floor-to-ceiling height of four metres (just over 13 feet). Originally built as a private home, the house was converted into a dental practice but has now been returned to its former use.

Müller was determined not be straight-jacketed by what he calls 'the historical corset' that can often restrict the modelling of a listed property. The client wanted the space to operate as a functional family home with a robust interior that would allow him to drive his motorbike easily into main hall. Here, the motorbike sits against a backdrop of white space and artworks.

The L-shaped plan wraps around a garden. Both wings open out onto the garden and accommodate the living space and kitchen/dining room areas. The shallow plan allows for views onto the canal and rear garden. As restrictions meant that the internal circulation could not be altered, the architect decided to introduce a network of sightlines by creating openings in the interior walls. These not only allow varying views but create a sense of connection between the wings. To reinforce the permanent quality of the building, robust floor materials such as slate tiles and oak floors were chosen.

◂ THE ARCHITECT WANTED THE INTERIOR FINISHES TO BE AS ROBUST AS POSSIBLE TO ALLOW THE CLIENT TO BE ABLE TO RIDE HIS BIKE DIRECTLY FROM THE STREET INTO THE HALL.

◄ DUE TO PLANNING RESTRICTIONS NO
INTERNAL WALLS COULD BE REMOVED.
THE ARCHITECT'S SOLUTION FOR
OPENING UP SIGHTLINES WITHIN THE
INTERIOR WAS TO CREATE FRAMED,
GLAZED OPENINGS THROUGHOUT THE
GROUND FLOOR.

HOUSE 10Kv SITS on a dominant site on the idyllic island of Lampedusa, overlooking the island's principal bay area. Lampedusa is the main island of the Pelagie archipelago, 200 kilometres (124 miles) southwest of Sicily and 113 kilometres (70 miles) from the Tunisian coast.

Before 1843 Lampedusa was uninhabited. Even today it has only one town, also called Lampedusa, with a population of 4,000, situated on the southeast point near the recently enlarged airport. The island is an increasingly popular tourist destination for Italians from the mainland and, in summertime, its population more than doubles. The island supports a traditional way of life based mainly on fishing. Its rugged aesthetic arises from its rocky shoreline and lack of trees. At the beginning of the last century, the island was completely deforested by prisoners of the jail established there, and a replanting programme has not yet been implemented. Buildings are mainly of local stone and brick.

Angelo Catania (after working in the office of Enric Miralles and Benedetta Tagliabue in Barcelona) was approached by the electricity supplier SELIS with the rare opportunity to convert one of their electricity sub-stations on the island of Lampedusa. The electricity supplier had decided to convert a series of disused sub-stations that previously converted up to 10,000 volts, hence the name 10Kv.

◀ THE FORMER ELECTRICITY SUB-STATION (SHOWN HERE IN ITS ORIGINAL STATE) HAD BEEN DISUSED AND POORLY MAINTAINED FOR A NUMBER OF YEARS.

▼ FROM LEFT: PLANS OF THE GROUND AND MEZZANINE LEVELS. THE GROUND FLOOR IS RESERVED FOR LIVING SPACE, KITCHEN AND BATHROOM, WHILE THE MEZZANINE ACCOMMODATES SLEEPING AREAS.

▶ THE RED-AND-WHITE BUILDING IS A DISTINCTIVE LANDMARK ABOVE LAMPEDUSA HARBOUR.

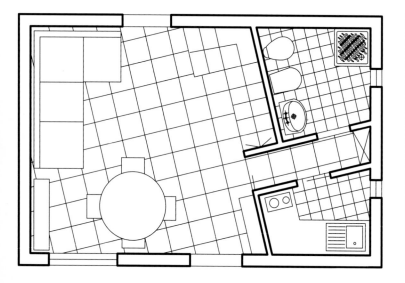

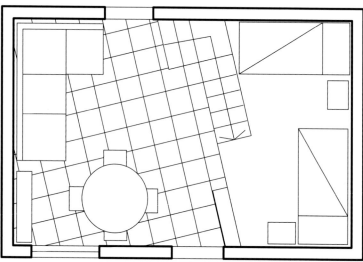

HOUSE 10KV

Angelo Catania

Lampedusa

Italy

The small units, with a footprint of approximately 7 × 4 metres (23 × 13 feet), are to be promoted as holiday apartments, and 10Kv is situated on one of the most spectacular points of the island, in between the marina and the Guitgia beach.

Internally, a steel frame supported all the electrical elements. High salt content in the air had caused the reinforcement bars to rust within the cast in-situ concrete structure. All internal fixtures were stripped out, leaving the concrete shell, which has a generous floor-to-ceiling height of 4.5 metres (14 feet 4 inches). The cabin was rendered and painted with bold vertical stripes in red and white, giving it a strong identity among the other coastal buildings of local stone. Red was chosen as a reference to the building's history, as the colour used for the high-voltage cables.

The internal space has been divided in an economic manner. A platform, which provides the sleeping area, has the access stair built into the dividing wall, behind which the kitchen and bathroom are housed. Guests can admire the sea views from the rooftop terrace, accessed by an external staircase.

KENTARO YAMAMOTO WAS a core member of the design and architecture group teledesign until he left in late 2005 to manage architecture studio Ka DESIGN. His previous projects include the skin-system house, a prototype for low-cost construction that uses a traditional Japanese module with a steel structural main frame and light steel sub-frame.

Yamamoto's transformation of a warehouse on a cramped site in Tokyo into a family home started with a phone call from a photographer who wanted a live/work studio and who asked: 'I wonder if I can live in the old store house?' Although this is not such an uncommon proposition in Europe, in Japan the common procedure has been to 'scrap and build', demolishing any structure that has outlived its function. However, a new drive towards building renovation is gradually gathering pace, especially in the cities.

With a canal that leads to the marine harbour running parallel to the site, the warehouse is situated on the east side of Tokyo. While the area is still largely industrial, regeneration of the harbour zone is progressing rapidly. The intention was to maintain the simplicity and dynamism of the original warehouse, a basic two-floored, pitched roof building constructed using a slim steel A-frame with industrial-sized garage gates on the ground-floor level. Yamamoto inserted a series of boxes that contain a bedroom, bathroom and dark room, built using FRP (Fibre

▶ THE TWO-STOREY WAREHOUSE (SHOWN HERE IN ITS ORIGINAL STATE) IS SITUATED IN AN AREA OF TOKYO OF MIXED LIGHT-INDUSTRIAL AND RESIDENTIAL PROPERTY.

▼ FROM LEFT: PLANS OF THE GROUND AND UPPER LEVELS. 1. GARAGE, 2. STUDIO, 3. BATHROOM, 4. WC, 5. STORE ROOM, 6. LIVING AREA, 7. DINING AREA, 8. BEDROOM, 9. WORK SPACE

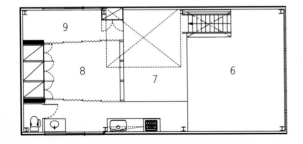

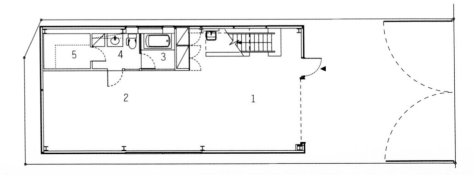

▸ THE A-FRAME STRUCTURE WAS
STRIPPED OF ITS CORRUGATED STEEL
CLADDING AND BREEZEBLOCK INFILL
AND THEN A NEW ALUMINIUM AND ZINC
CLADDING WITH INSULATION WAS
CONSTRUCTED.

▲ THE UPPER-LEVEL LIVING AND DINING AREAS ARE SEPARATED FROM THE BEDROOM BY AN OPAQUE SCREEN WHICH ALLOWS LIGHT TO PENETRATE THE ENTIRE SPACE.

◀ THE UPPER LEVEL BEFORE CONVERSION.

▶ THE GROUND-LEVEL GARAGE IN ITS ORIGINAL STATE.

Reinforced Plastics). During the day the bedroom box allows rays of sunlight to filter through the skin, transmitting light into the space. At night the box provides a beacon of light. The building's external skin was clad with zinc and aluminium. An internal wall houses thermal insulation to ensure that the warehouse meets domestic thermal standards.

▲ A FOLDING GLASS SCREEN ATTACHED TO THE END OF THE BEDROOM STORAGE UNIT CAN BE EXTENDED TO SEPARATE OFF THE ADJACENT WORK SPACE.

▼ THE CONCRETE SCREED FLOOR WAS RETAINED IN THE LOWER-LEVEL STUDIO. THE BATHROOM IS HOUSED IN THE ILLUMINATED BOX ON THE LEFT.

GALLOP RESIDENCE

Lacina Heitler Architects/The Apartment Creative Agency

New York

USA

▲ THE SIXTH FLOOR OF THIS FORMER YMCA BUILDING (SHOWN HERE BEFORE CONVERSION) HAS A GENEROUS FLOOR SPACE OF 325 SQUARE METRES (3,500 SQUARE FEET).

▲ THE BLACK MOSAIC-TILED KITCHEN WITH THE LIBRARY BEYOND. THE DESIGN OF THE GERRIT RIETVELD CHAIR WAS CUSTOMIZED TO FIT IN WITH THE DARK COLOUR SCHEME OF THE SPACE BY REMOVING THE PRIMARY COLOURS FROM THE SURFACE, LEAVING JUST THE RED TO EMPHASIZE THE PLANES.

◄ THE OWNER'S COLLECTION OF ANTIQUE AND COLONIAL FURNISHINGS, WHICH INCLUDES CHAISES LONGUES, PLANTER'S CHAIRS AND LEOPARD SKINS, ALL CONTRIBUTE TO THE APARTMENT'S SENSE OF DRAMA AND THEATRICALITY.

WHEN LACINA HEITLER ARCHITECTS and interior design firm The Apartment Creative Agency were contacted by Cindy Gallop to design her 325 square metre (3,500 square foot) apartment in New York, they knew that it would be no conventional domestic retreat. Gallop's brief was succinct and specific: 'At midnight I want to feel like I am in a Shanghai nightclub.' The designers responded with what they called 'a vision of the night': 'We didn't expect her to go with this, an entirely black apartment, but she did!'

Cindy Gallop is no shrinking violet; she has carved out an illustrious career in advertising and was voted USA Advertising Woman of the Year 2003. After working for Bartle Bogle Hegarty, one of Britain's leading advertising agencies in London and Singapore, she fronted the company's move to New York. After only four years the agency was voted *Adweek*'s 2002 Eastern Agency of the Year. Described as the fast-talking president with a pinch of the rock star, owing to her leather and feathers wardrobe, Cindy Gallop wanted an apartment interior that would mirror her personal style.

The apartment is situated in a former YMCA building in Manhattan's fashionable Chelsea district, and the client wanted it to be a showcase for her life. Within the sixth-floor space - originally the men's showers and locker rooms - there are no dividing walls. Instead, a series of sheer, black curtains with an underlayer of soundproof material can be drawn to achieve room division and a moiré effect. With nominal divisions, the apartment is laid out to comprise a kitchen and library area and a series of gallery spaces. The client is a keen art collector and the walls are adorned with an eclectic mix of art ranging from a Gucci studded chain saw to antique wall mirrors. To further reinforce the theatrical effect, the bathtub is placed on a stage where Gallop can view her surrounds. With echoes of the Philippines' former First Lady Imelda Marcos, an elegant shelf display placed along one of the walls in the main living space unit shows off Gallop's 250 pairs of shoes. Two bathrooms, divided from the main space with partition walls, provide the only reprieve from the nocturnal interior.

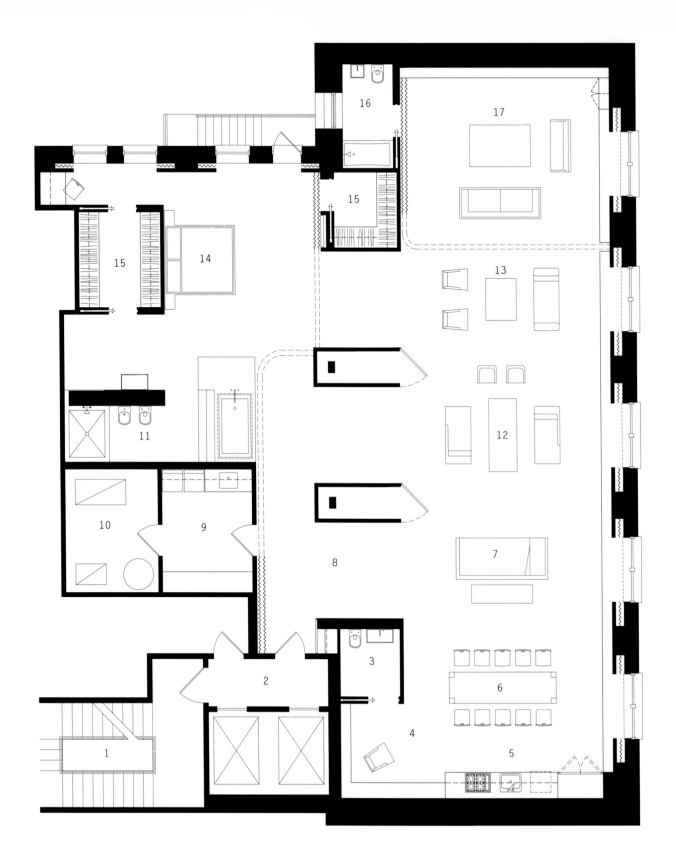

◂ PLAN OF THE APARTMENT.
1. STAIR, 2. ELEVATOR LOBBY,
3. WC, 4. LIBRARY, 5. KITCHEN,
6. DINING, 7. GALLERY THREE,
8. ENTRANCE, 9 & 10. MECHANICAL
ROOM, 11. MASTER BATHROOM,
12. GALLERY TWO, 13. GALLERY ONE,
14. MASTER BEDROOM, 15. MASTER
CLOSET, 16. BATHROOM, 17. TV ROOM

▸ THE MOSAIC-TILED MASTER BATH,
SITUATED IN THE MIDDLE OF THE
LIVING SPACE, GIVES A DIFFERENT
DIMENSION TO BATHING.

▾ THE MASTER BEDROOM. TO PROVIDE
PRIVACY WHEN NEEDED, HEAVY
CURTAINS - MADE OF A SOUND PROOF
FABRIC FROM A THEATRICAL SUPPLIER
- ARE RUN ON CONCEALED TRACKS.

OVERLEAF: A ROW OF TOM DIXON GLOBE
LIGHTS ENHANCES THE 'SHANGHAI
NIGHTCLUB' ATMOSPHERE OF THE MAIN
LIVING SPACE.

WORKSHOP HOUSE
Nathalie Wolberg

◀ THE STEEL RIBBON STAIRCASE
LEADS UP TO THE TERRACE AND ACTS
AS A RETREAT, ENCOURAGING
OCCUPANTS TO USE THE TREADS AS
SEATS.

▾ FROM BOTTOM: PLANS OF THE
BASEMENT, GROUND AND FIRST FLOOR.
1. ENTRANCE, 2. SPACE FOR
RELAXING, 3. KITCHEN/DINING,
4. READING AREA, 5. SUSPENDED
NET, 6. WASHING, 7. SLEEPING,
8. EXHIBITION SPACE, 9. WORKING
SPACE, 10. TERRACE

▾ THE WAREHOUSE WAS FORMERLY
A PRINTING WORKS BUILT IN THE
1950s, WITH STEEL-FRAMED WINDOWS
AND CONCRETE, LOAD-BEARING WALLS.

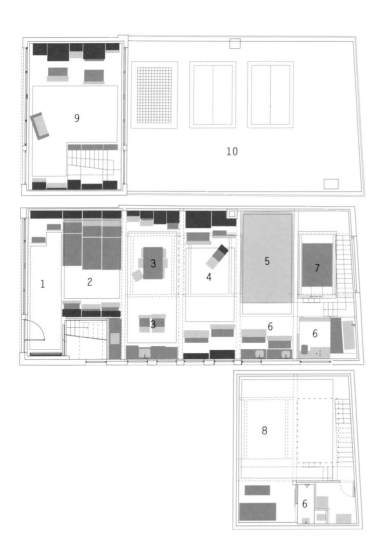

AS PROPERTY PRICES continue to rise in the centre of Paris, artists' quarters have started to spring up around the city's *banlieux*. Nathalie Wolberg decided to locate her studio and home in Saint-Ouen, north of Paris's centre and situated close to the famous Saint-Ouen flea market. With excellent transport connections into Paris and the advantage of living in tree-lined streets neighbouring a large park, Saint-Ouen is increasingly becoming a popular artists' colony.

Wolberg, an interior architect with a background in theatre design, wanted to explore a blueprint for living, which she describes as a type of 'domestic typology'. The home is situated in the former offices of a printing works factory dating back to the 1950s, which has been converted into nine artists' workshops. Each individual unit is approximately 180 square metres (1,900 square feet). Wolberg's unit also has the luxury of an 80 square metre (860 square foot) terrace.

True to the Modernist doctrine that space can contribute to the inhabitant's well being, she explored the unit as a laboratory of ideas and refuge for relaxation. With her experience in theatre design she constructed a narrative that would 'engender an architecture with affective and erotic dimensions', treating the space as a series of moving stage sets. These moveable rooms can be arranged in different configurations to form the backdrop for a variety of

social situations. Large, open spaces give way to
areas of intimacy while allowing sightlines to link up
throughout the space.

The concrete-framed warehouse was overlaid with
partitions and framed structures, so that the space
would read as a series of bays. Each unit, constructed
out of timber studding and welded steel frames, was
detailed to the highest level. Stepping over the
threshold of the house the entrance hall becomes a
chamber, acting as a transitional strip between the
inside and the outside. From the hall, a staircase of
rounded steps constructed of steel strips leads to the
workshop, which gives access onto a terrace. The
staircase, with its unusual steps, has become a place
to sit and enjoy views across the terrace.

After passing the second bay the space opens up into
the main living area, integrating different environments such as dining and cooking. The large net
suspended from the existing void acts as a dynamic
intervention, which Wolberg describes as a space for
the 'body to assume its own gravity'. Following the
perimeter of the space, more intimate functional areas
such as reading desks and washrooms have been inserted
behind furniture doors. In varying widths, colours and
angles, the doors produce a dynamic asymmetry that
breaks up the repetition of the dividers. Low tables
have intergrated seating that can be rolled out. The
bedroom is designed so that the main visual vantage

point affords views over the living space, but it can
be enclosed with a series of screens and blinds. At the
far end of the main living area, a staircase with cantilevered treads leads down to a double-height space
in which the net is suspended and light penetrates
through large glass windows. This is currently used as
an exhibition space.

An integrated lighting programme uses translucent
canvas partitions and concealed ceiling lights. Each
bay includes four different types of lighting, which
enables the ambience of the house to be moderated end-
lessly. The role of artificial light is to complement
natural daylight. Depending on different activities
taking place in the house, the light generates appro-
priate ambiences, based on coloured or non-coloured,
diffused or concentrated lights.

Described by Wolberg as 'an object of pleasure and
desire', the result is a highly sensual space, which
acts much like a kaleidoscopic receptor of changing
light and colour patterns.

◄ HAND BASINS FOR VISITORS ARE
HUNG FROM THE LIGHTING PANELS AND
CAN BE CONCEALED BY MOVEABLE
WALLS ON RUNNERS.

▸ THE SUSPENDED NET PROVIDES 14
SQUARE METRES (150 SQUARE FEET)
OF SPACE TO LOUNGE IN. THE VOID
WAS PART OF THE ORIGINAL FACTORY
STRUCTURE.

▴ WOLBERG HAS INTRODUCED A SERIES
OF SCREENS THAT PULL DOWN FROM
CONCEALED REVEALS IN THE CEILING
SPACE AND WHICH ARE DOWNLIT WITH
FLUSHES OF COLOURED LIGHTING.

▸ THE FURNITURE IS SEAMLESSLY
INTEGRATED WITH THE ARCHITECTURE:
IN THIS CASE STEEL RIBBON TABLES
SEEM TO BE EXTRUDED FROM THE
FLOOR.

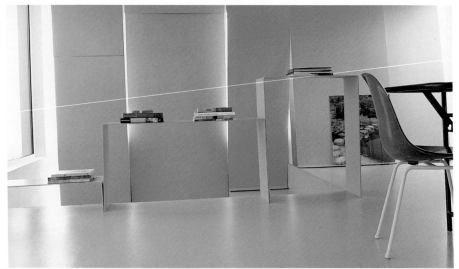

LOFT STUDIO

Manuel Serrano Arquitectos

Madrid

Spain

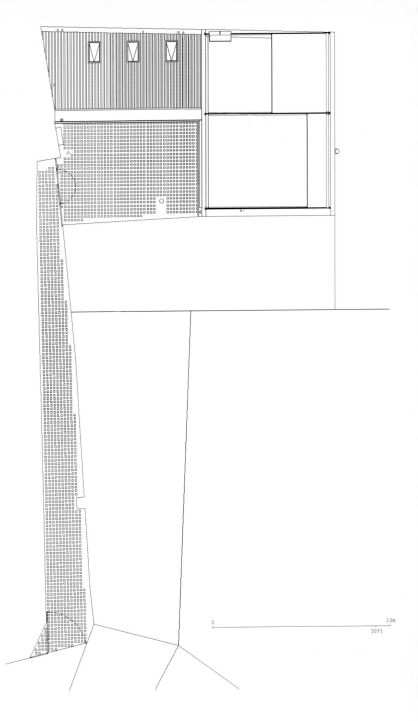

▲ SITE PLAN, SHOWING THE PATHWAY
AND COURTYARD ON THE LEFT.

◀ THE MAIN, DOUBLE-HEIGHT LIVING
SPACE IS OVERLOOKED BY A STEEL
MEZZANINE. SERVICES ARE VISIBLY
APPLIED TO THE UNPLASTERED BRICK
WALLS.

0   10m
                  30ft

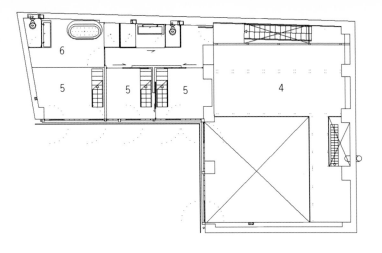

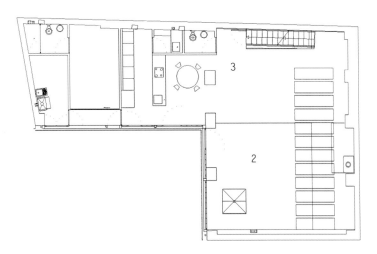

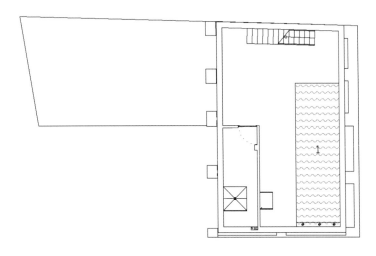

MANUEL SERRANO ARQUITECTOS was asked to apply an industrial aesthetic to the run down buildings that the clients, a couple with three children, had purchased in the centre of Madrid. The buildings, former sculpture workshops, formed a rather ad hoc collection of one- and two-storey workshops within the yard of a residential block. The clients requested a space that could be adapted for many uses, above all entertaining on a large scale, and also asked that a pool be integrated into the interior. The pool was situated in the lower ground floor as the client did not want it to become a dominant feature in the main living area. Instead, the intention was that occupants would be made aware of the pool when moving through the space by the sound of the water and the light reflecting off the water and bouncing around the building.

In order to bring some cohesion to the buildings, the architects rationalized the space by constructing a courtyard to the rear of the site so that it would not be overlooked by neighbouring buildings. The architects describe the structure as 'a vertical city garden' that rewrites the history of the building, not merely a renovation but a remodelling of the space to give it a contemporary function.

The external walls, which make up the courtyard façade, have large, glazed sliding doors and U-glass. To give the façade a formal unity it was clad

▲ THE WAREHOUSE BEFORE
CONVERSION.

◄ FROM BOTTOM: PLANS OF THE
BASEMENT, GROUND AND UPPER
LEVELS. 1. POOL, 2. LIVING AREA,
3. KITCHEN/DINING AREA,
4. MEZZANINE STUDY, 5. BEDROOM,
6. BATHROOM

▲▸THE HIGH-TECH STAINLESS-STEEL
KITCHEN IS LOCATED JUST OFF THE
LIVING AREA AND HAS GLASS DOORS TO
ONE SIDE THAT OPEN OUT ONTO THE
COURTYARD.

◂ FURNISHINGS ARE DESIGNED TO BE
EITHER MOVEABLE OR HAVE THE
ABILITY TO BE REASSEMBLED,
ALLOWING A GREAT DEAL OF
FLEXIBILITY WITHIN THE LIVING
SPACE.

▾ THE TOUGHENED-GLASS CEILING OF
THE LOWER-GROUND FLOOR POOL
ALLOWS LIGHT TO PASS THROUGH FROM
ABOVE, WHILE ALSO BOUNCING
REFLECTIONS OFF THE WATER BACK UP
TO THE MAIN LIVING AREA.

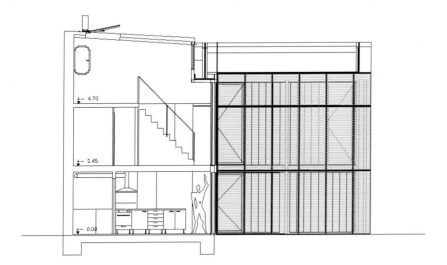

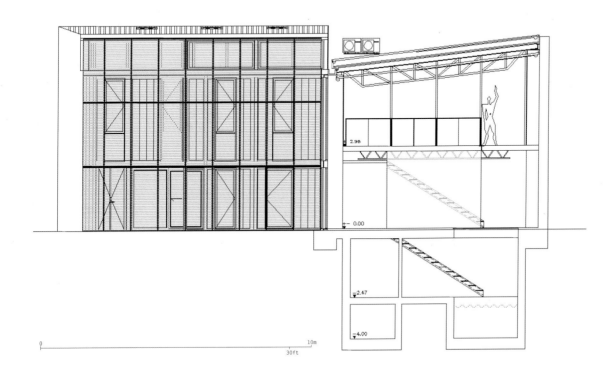

with aluminium and perforated-steel panels that allow the light to filter into the interior.

The interior layout is described by the architects as 'throwing into question the standardized norms of domesticity'. The swimming pool, which was constructed within cast-concrete, loadbearing walls, also helps to support the original brick walls above. The ceiling of the pool comprises a series of concrete beams with glazed openings of toughened glass. This creates a transparent floor area for the ground floor, providing a visual sightline between the pool and the ground-floor living space above.

Steel trusses support the mezzanine level above the ground floor, and a balcony space runs around the perimeter. Offset from the living area is the kitchen – a stainless-steel laboratory for cooking – from which glass doors slide open to access the external courtyard. On warm days the whole house opens out, bringing daylight into the building. The architects describe the furniture as part of the philosphy of the building; it is either moveable on castors or employs systems that allow it to be demounted and reassembled. All services are run visably up the original brick walls as no internal plastering was introduced. During construction, insulation was packed onto the outside walls and the U-glass on the courtyard side provides sufficient insulation both in summer and winter.

BOGENALLEE APARTMENTS

blauraum architekten

◄ THE CONVERSION OF THIS 1970s OFFICE BUILDING IN THE CENTRE OF HAMBURG (SHOWN HERE IN ITS ORIGINAL STATE) IS TYPICAL OF AN ONGOING URBAN REGENERATION TREND FOR CONVERTING REDUNDANT OFFICE SPACE IN THE CITY CENTRE INTO RESIDENTIAL UNITS.

▼ THE ARCHITECTS HAVE ADDED A DYNAMIC, WOOD-CLAD STREET FAÇADE ARTICULATED WITH EXTRUDED BOXES THAT HOUSE DINING SPACES AND BATHROOMS.

THE YOUNG ARCHITECTURAL PRACTICE blauraum was established in 2002 in Hamburg, and is forging ahead with an impressive list of creative projects and established clients. Not content with pushing their role as designers, the architects have also set up the blauraum gallery. Their exhibition programme boasts a diverse cultural platform, which acts as a forum and showcase for the work of other practices, exploring contemporary themes in architecture, design and urbanism.

German development company, Cogiton, which has a track record of working with talented architects and an awareness of the benefits a strong design identity can bring, approached blauraum to work on one of its projects in Hamburg. The city of Hamburg is experiencing a flowering of urban regeneration. Its harbour area, once a seedy, ungentrified quarter, is now the focus of a large, mixed-use development. Bogenallee, which is situated near the regeneration area in the Hamburg-Harvestehude district, plays a part in this resurgence. The brief invited the architects to devise a scheme to convert a concrete-framed office building, built in 1974, into a residential block.

The original office building, with parking on the ground floor, was stripped of its rear and front façades and a different façade concept was realized for each. In all, 15 apartments with varying floor areas from 83 square metres (893 square feet) to 144

▸▸ AN EXTRUDED 'FLEXBOX' HOUSES A BATHROOM WITH FULL-LENGTH SLIDING GLASS DOORS.

▸ THE REAR FAÇADE FOLLOWS THE PRINCIPAL OF EXTRUDING THE FLOOR PLANE – INTRODUCED ON THE FRONT FAÇADE – TO CREATE AN ADDITIONAL BALCONY AREA.

▾ SECTION WITH THE STREET FAÇADE TO THE LEFT AND THE REAR GARDEN FAÇADE TO THE RIGHT.

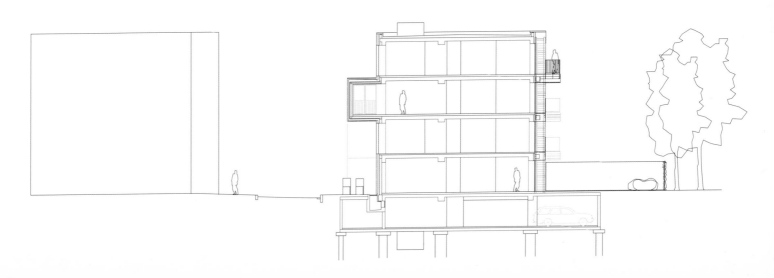

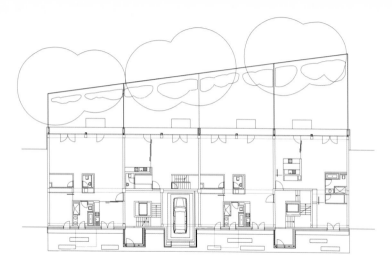

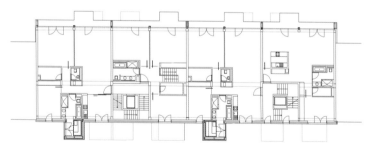

0 5m 10m
15ft 30ft

▲ FROM LEFT: GROUND-FLOOR AND
FIRST-FLOOR PLANS. THE GARDEN
TERRACES AND BALCONIES ARE AT THE
TOP, THE STREET FAÇADE AT THE
BOTTOM.

▸ THE EXISTING COLUMN-AND-BEAM
STRUCTURE HAS BEEN EXPRESSED
RATHER THAN CONCEALED UNDER FALSE
CEILINGS.

▸▸ KITCHEN FITTINGS ARE LOCATED
ALONG ONE INNER WALL TO ALLOW
SPACE FOR A DINING AREA.

◄ THE INTERIORS HAVE NO INTERNAL PARTITION WALLS EXCEPT FOR THE BOXES THAT HOUSE THE KITCHENS AND BATHROOM AREAS.

square metres (1,550 square feet) have been designed to accommodate both families and single occupants.

For the main façade facing the street, a quiet cul-de-sac, the architects have used what they term 'Flexboxes', which resemble drawers pulled out and protruding at the same lengths. The boxes allow for extensions of the kitchen, living area, bedroom or bathroom, providing space for additions such as a dining table, bath or sauna. All of the boxes are punctuated with floor-to-ceiling windows to the left or right side. The rear façade is largely opened up with large bands of glazing providing views onto the private garden area. Terraces run the length of the glazing with extruded balconies running perpendicular to the façade. Each individual flat façade has a different composition that is a variant of the same theme. By avoiding repetition, a dynamic effect is achieved.

Largely open plan, the internal space has room dividers that also act as storage and shelving. The only contained areas are the units that house the kitchen and the bathroom.

The apartments have contributed a sense of drama to the street front, while playing with the more prosaic framework of the urban villa. In 2005 the project was awarded a Deutscher Architekturpreis Commendation in recognition of its contribution to a new urban architecture.

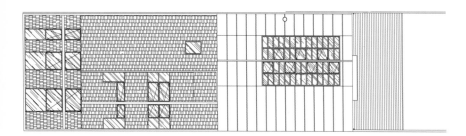

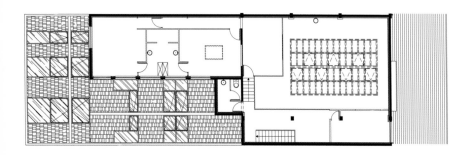

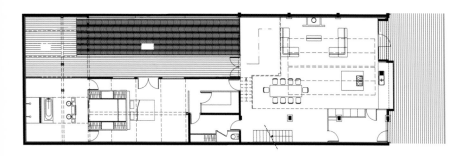

▲ FROM BOTTOM: GROUND-, FIRST-
AND ROOF-LEVEL PLANS.

ALEXANDRE BARTHÉLEMY AND STEPHANIE IFRAH met at the School of Architecture in Paris and after working for various architectural firms decided to establish their own practice based in the western Parisian suburb of Colombes, near La Défense. A steady stream of projects - both interior fit outs and new-builds - in the residential market has allowed them to develop their own version of rationalist architecture. Ifrah describes their architectural mission as 'focusing on the design of neutral spaces on to which the client can prescribe their own use'.

The architects were commissioned by a Parisian couple, who run a restaurant in the city centre, to design a house that would provide a refuge from their hectic life. The clients' dream was to have an indoor swimming pool. Working within a fairly tight budget, the architects urged the clients not to lose sight of their original idea as other design features were pared down to enable enough funds to be dedicated to the pool area. The building, situated on a narrow, linear site in Colombes, was formerly a small industrial unit that had recently operated as a model-making workshop. In order to obtain planning permission it was decided to keep the existing structure without making any changes to the volume or building height. The two-storey building is constructed of a simple, steel-truss pitched roof.

▲ THE DOUBLE-HEIGHT LIVING SPACE
IS LIT FROM ABOVE BY A GENEROUS
SERIES OF ROOFLIGHTS.

Excited by the prospect of this unusual domestic typology, the architects decided that the pool would become the central feature around which the other functions would sit, as well as becoming the driving aesthetic element. Ifrah talks of 'creating a space that would be enlivened by this crystalline blue surface sending shafts of light through the interior'.

The main space of the building is a double-height volume, which was designed to accommodate the living area. A mezzanine balcony provides the circulation to the bedrooms. The pool runs parallel to the site walls adjacent to the main living area on the ground floor. The pool is fitted with a salt filtration system as an alternative to chlorine, which can erode concrete surfaces.

Adjacent to the pool are the main bedroom and bathrooms, fitted out in a raw-looking palette of materials such as rough-grained wood and concrete screeded floors. The clients talk about the luxury of stepping in to the pool area on the way to the kitchen, stopping for a quick dip before coffee and croissants.

▲ THE LACK OF DIVIDING WALLS IN THE BATHROOM ALLOWS LIGHT TO FLOOD THE SPACE. PRIVACY IS PROVIDED BY WOOD 'BOXES'. THE POOL IS ON THE OTHER SIDE OF A GLASS WALL (LEFT).

▼ FROM LEFT: LONG AND SHORT SECTIONS THROUGH THE FACTORY. THE DOUBLE-HEIGHT LIVING AREA IS TO THE LEFT OF THE LONG SECTION.

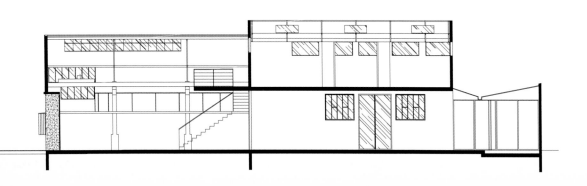

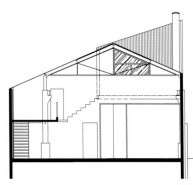

▲ THOUGH THE BUDGET WAS LIMITED,
THE CLIENTS' MAIN STIPULATION WAS
THAT THE CONVERSION SHOULD
INCLUDE AN INDOOR SWIMMING POOL.

▶ THE MAIN BEDROOM IS SEPARATED
FROM THE BATHROOM BY A LARGE
WOODEN BOX – RATHER THAN A
DIVIDING WALL – SO AS NOT TO
IMPEDE THE FLOW OF LIGHT.

3

LOFTS

ICE HOUSE LOFTS
Rob Paulus Architect

ESTABLISHED IN 1995, Rob Paulus Architect has designed a wide range of buildings. Having grown up in the desert, Paulus sites the large expanse of rugged nature as a strong influence on the way that he constructs buildings.

The Ice House Lofts comprise 51 distinctive residences located in the 1923 Arizona Ice and Cold Storage Company building, an ice manufacturing plant that closed in 2002. The triangular site posed certain constraints. At the back it is hemmed in with heavy transport arteries, the Union Pacific Rails and Aviation Parkway. Therefore the building is orientated to the front, where a pool with pool house has been constructed for the residents. The conversion is a successful example of tapping into an existing infrastructure within an urban infill area to establish a pattern of what is termed 'Smart Growth' by the developer, appropriately named Deep Freeze Development.

'Smart Growth' has become the intelligent answer to the problem of urban sprawl, and has gathered momentum as a movement. A group made up of environmentalists, planners and preservationists advocate a set of land use and design strategies although, with the exception of New Urbanism, one with no ideal physical form. The movement is intended to direct new development towards existing urbanized areas and away from agricultural and natural landscapes. In the conversion of the Ice

▲ THE SOUTH ELEVATION BEFORE (TOP) AND AFTER CONVERSION (ABOVE). SENSITIVE RENOVATION ENSURED THAT THE BUILDING'S CHARACTERISTIC AND VARIED FAÇADE WAS LEFT INTACT.

▼ CROSS-SECTION SHOWING TWO FLOORS OF SPLIT-LEVEL UNITS. THE SOUTH ELEVATION IS ON THE LEFT.

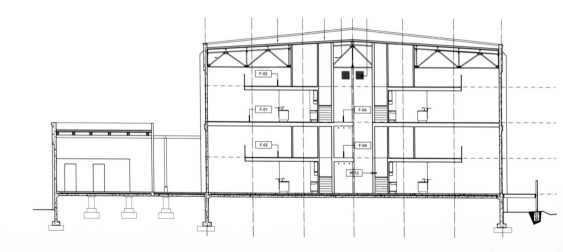

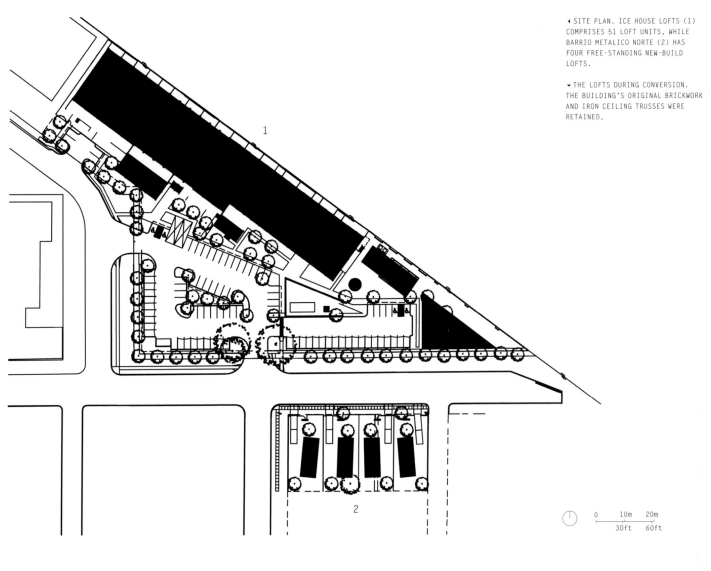

1

2

| 0 | 10m | 20m |
| 30ft | 60ft |

House Lofts, the renovation of the existing industrial building and the salvaging of materials demonstrate a consideration of environmental factors. For example, 1,524 metres (5,000 feet) of 2 × 10 timber, 1,340 square metres (14,400 square feet) of corrugated metal and eight kilometres (five miles) of salvaged shiplap wood were creatively incorporated into the lofts. Other details, such as salvaged wheel hands, were reused as gate entry handles, while old machinery was sandblasted for use as sculptural elements, all adding to the reading of the building's history. The building's surface is enriched with varying textures, including exposed concrete and the massive wood beams and riveted steel trusses that contrast with the new design interventions. Requiring a sensitive collaborative process with city planners, officials, consultants and contractors, the project's success has contributed to the regeneration of a once run-down area in downtown Tucson.

◄ BARE CONCRETE WALLS AND MASSIVE BEAMS CONTINUE THE INDUSTRIAL AESTHETIC INSIDE THE APARTMENTS.

▾ LOWER-LEVEL PLAN OF A TYPICAL SPLIT-LEVEL UNIT. 1. KITCHEN, 2. LIVING AREA, 3. BATHROOM, 4. VOID, 5. DECK

▾ ▾ THE TYPICAL SPLIT-LEVEL UNIT HAS A KITCHEN UNDERNEATH THE MEZZANINE, WHICH IS REACHED BY AN IRON DOUBLE STAIRCASE.

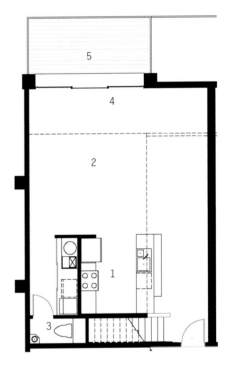

‹ THE FABRIC DYE WAREHOUSE
EXTERIOR BEFORE CONVERSION.

› THE EXTERIOR AFTER CONVERSION.
THE BRICKWORK WAS COVERED IN
CONCRETE RENDER, WHILE TOUGH-
LOOKING GRILLS AT STREET LEVEL
COMPLETES THE RAW EFFECT OF THE
FINISH.

WHEN THE MEMBERS OF the Australian architecture practice Dale Jones-Evans Pty Ltd Architecture decided that they had out-grown their present office, they made a unanimous decision to design their own space. Having built up a diverse portfolio of architecture and interior projects, from exquisitely detailed interiors to efficient office fit-outs, and inspirational single and multiple residential projects, including adaptive re-use, they decided to apply this commercial experience to self-financing their own building project.

The first step was to find a former dye factory situated in the Surry Hills area of Sydney. They then sought planning permission to convert the building into nine residential lofts and office space. Surry Hills has a diverse past, which is still very much in evidence today. In the early nineteenth century, it was a small village on the outskirts of Sydney where the affluent classes built sizeable villas. By the 1850s, the area expanded with speculative developers building rows of elegant Victorian terraces. The area then sank into decline, becoming an overcrowded slum, with brothels, illicit grog shops and notorious gangs. In the early 1900s, the suburb was home to a large Chinese community due to its proximity to the markets. However, much of this community was driven out by the slum clearances and road widening undertaken by the council between 1906 and 1929. Post-

▾FROM BOTTOM: PLANS OF THE GROUND
FLOOR, FIRST-FLOOR MEZZANINE AND
SECOND FLOOR.

war migration brought many Europeans, particularly from Greece and Italy, to the area, who were attracted to the low-cost housing. Today's Surry Hills is a colourful suburb, a far cry from its shady past, and well known for art galleries, antique dealers, cafés, pubs and fashion outlets.

Bound by three streets, the 1920s factory consisted of a concrete-frame construction with masonry infill. Parts of the masonry brickwork were stripped out on the ground floor and on the upper floors to open up the façade and allow light to flood into the building. The envelope of the building was maintained while removing the lower floor so as to insert two-storey mezzanine floors across the new floor plate. To create three storey, upper penthouse apartments, the existing first floor was maintained and re-loaded with two additional floors. This combination created the possibility for a diversity of housing types, sizes and styles within the development. Spacious raw and bunker type lofts stud the street while the penthouse apartments penetrate through the old envelope above.

A generous entrance passage with stairwell contains two flights of stairs, mirroring each other in a baroque gesture. The stairs are built using robust materials such as cast in-situ concrete and galvanized steel. This approach, described by the architects as 'hard core', arose from the proposal to

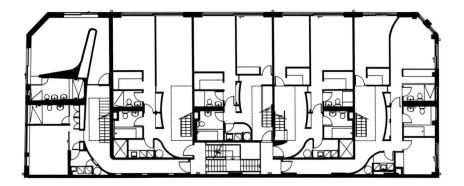

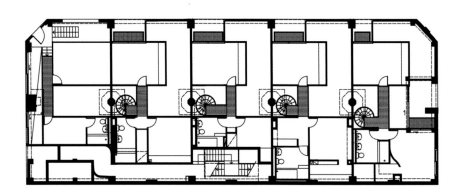

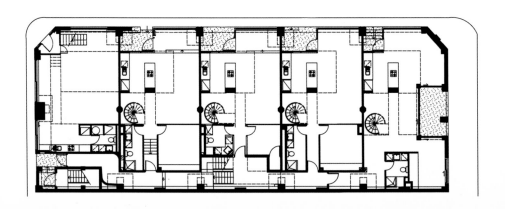

bring the streetscape into the building and accentuate the contradiction entailed by such a move. Security grillage, used on the doors and windows, provides a secure entrance hall and the introduction of massive windows creates increased two-way surveillance.

Throughout the lower shell, a series of suspended box-like insertions were added. These steel-framed boxes are suspended by metal angles and cables from the remaining upper floor slab, with the spaces trimmed in steel and clad with plasterboard. The boxes appear to float over the ground floor in the spectacular raw concrete apartment shells, which have a floor-to-ceiling height of 5.5 metres (18 feet).

The building's monastic appearance disguises a more sensual and spatially complex composition of gallery-type interior spaces. Where possible, the existing concrete has been grit blasted and left unpainted as a reference to the building's industrial past. The

▲ LEFT: LOOKING UP THE STAIRS TO THE MEZZANINE LEVEL IN A PENTHOUSE APARTMENT.

▲ THE CHUNKY STEEL AND IN-SITU CAST CONCRETE STAIRWELL REFLECTS THE ARCHITECT'S 'HARD CORE' APPROACH, AND FEATURES A SPECIALLY COMMISSIONED ARTWORK BY AUSTRALIAN ARTIST SUSAN NORRIE.

penthouses have been designed with bamboo louvres and gives access onto a large roof terrace.

On other projects Dale Jones-Evans has worked closely with artists, either as a collaborative team or by introducing an artistic proposal to the design process. In 2002-2003, the practice developed the Art Wall, Kings Cross, a corner building in Sydney, which is wrapped in a delicate laser cut, patterned sunscreen. The building is crowned with a light box, which acts a huge canvas for public art works. For its innovative use of steel in architecture, the project was awarded the 2004 NSW RAIA Colorbond Steel Award.

For the project in Ann Street, the architects commissioned Barcelona installation artist Danni Marti and Australian contemporary painter Susan Norrie to create art works that reflect the industrial nature of the building. Norrie worked with the architects on a 15 metre (49 feet) high art work in the common stair. This consists of tens of layers of gloss oil-based glazes and paints, ranging from deep blood red at the bottom of the stairwell to sticky textured bituminous gloss black at the top where the light enters the building. Highly reflective, the surface forms a painterly mirror effect in which the reflections of passersby appear like ghosts.

▲ IN THE GROUND-FLOOR APARTMENTS THE STEEL-FRAMED BOX-LIKE MEZZANINES (TO THE RIGHT OF THE PICTURE) APPEAR TO FLOAT ABOVE THE SPACE.

▲ THE PENTHOUSE APARTMENTS,
WHICH OPEN ONTO THE ROOF TERRACE,
ARE CLAD WITH BAMBOO LOUVRES.

◄ THE ELEVATION FACING ONTO
LITTLE RILEY STREET. THE
BRICKWORK ON THE GROUND AND UPPER
FLOORS WAS STRIPPED OUT TO ALLOW
MORE LIGHT INTO THE APARTMENTS.

FLINDERS LANE APARTMENT

rice & skinner

Melbourne

Australia

◄ THE STUDY AREA IS TUCKED BEHIND
THE KITCHEN 'BOX', THE OUTER EDGE
OF WHICH IS SEEN ON THE LEFT OF
THE PHOTOGRAPH.

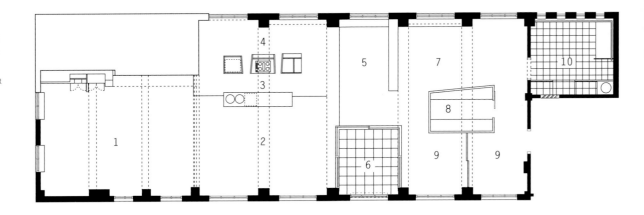

► PLAN. 1. LIVING ROOM, 2. DINING ROOM, 3. KITCHEN, 4. STUDY, 5. LIBRARY, 6. BALCONY, 7. MASTER BEDROOM, 8. WARDROBE, 9. BEDROOM, 10. BATHROOM

▼ THE INTERIOR OF THE OFFICE FLOOR BEFORE CONVERSION. WINDOWS ALONG THREE SIDES ALLOW A GREAT AMOUNT OF LIGHT INTO THE SPACE.

LOOKING FOR THAT RARE commodity, an unrenovated industrial space in the inner city area of Melbourne, the intention of rice & skinner architects was to design an interior that would act as a counterpoint to the density and congestion of urban life. They found a 1930s office building in the buzzing Flinders Lane quarter, once the centre of the garment trade, that provided an ideal shell. On the roof were two squash courts, now in a state of disrepair, that had belonged to the rag trade industry's club.

Focusing on creating a space where two people could live independently and together, the architects also wanted to provide accommodation for a guest without compromising the main living spaces. To achieve this, the partition walls were removed so that the architects could explore the notion of defining spaces by means of their particular functions. All functional equipment was stored in a series of boxes, which were then used to create divisions.

The building, which is freestanding with windows on three sides, benefits from natural light. Plans were introduced to enhance the horizontal planes and to introduce three boxes to define the internal space. Changes in level and varied use of materials articulate the planes. The boxes appear to be randomly placed in the space. One creates a kitchen area, with a study area tucked behind the kitchen wall providing a snug work environment. This box is constructed using

▾ THE MARBLE-CLAD BATHROOM IS THE
ONLY SPACE IN THE APARTMENT WITH A
DOOR (IN OPAQUE GLASS TO ALLOW
LIGHT THROUGH).

▸ THE SPACE WAS CONCEIVED AS A
SERIES OF PLANES AND BOXES THAT
FOCUS ON INDIVIDUAL FUNCTIONS
WITHOUT THE NEED FOR WALLS OR
DOORS.

plywood finishes with hoop pine (a sustainable timber native to Australia) veneer stained dark brown. The terrace area is defined by a glass box that protrudes into the middle of the apartment. When illuminated at night the box becomes a refraction device, mirroring and reflecting activity and light.

An interpretation of original loft living, the space has no dividers apart from the front door. The other exception is the full-height, partially opaque glass door to the bathroom, which creates a screen that still allows light to filter through.

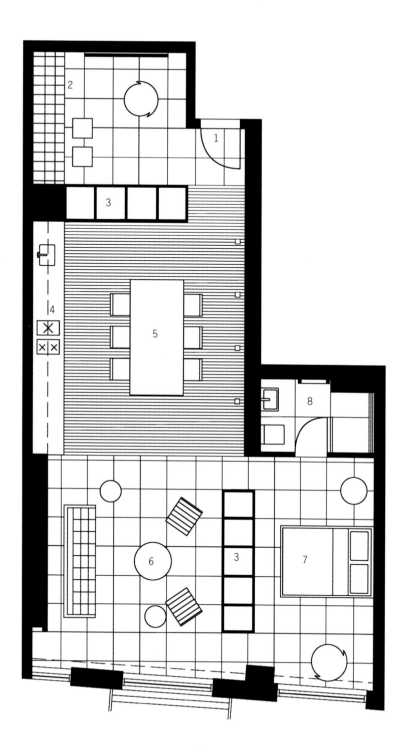

THE RED TULIP CHOCOLATE FACTORY stands in Prahran, an area of regeneration in the inner city of Melbourne. Formerly a factory specializing in the production of chocolate, the building has a wealth of striking industrial features. These include an expressed concrete frame with generous open-plan spaces and high ceilings. The original shell was well maintained, allowing the 100 square metre (1,076 square foot) floor area to be completed in just over three months.

David Hicks, the interior designer and client, turned the apartment into a showcase of minimalist living with discreet detailing and ambient lighting. A contemporary expression of the playboy's fantasy playpen, the space is finished in monochrome surfaces. Conceived as a grid formula, the floor plan is moderated by the size and layout of the white terrazzo floor tiles. The grid became the ordering principle for dividing the area into a series of zones with the interior furniture falling within them. This design approach was conceived after Hicks made a studied analysis of how his personal environment could be pared down to fit into the limited footprint of the apartment.

The L-shaped plan was lit only by a glazed south-facing façade, setting a design challenge as to how best to evoke a sense of extended space. Mirrors were placed along the longitudinal section and the generous 3.2 metre (10 foot) floor-to-ceiling height allowed a

◄ PLAN. 1. ENTRANCE. 2. FOLD-OUT BED. 3. STORAGE. 4. KITCHEN. 5. DINING AREA. 6. LIVING AREA. 7. BEDROOM. 8. BATHROOM

► THOUGH THE LIVING AND DINING SPACES ARE OPEN-PLAN, THE RAISED BLACK GLOSSY PLATFORM PROVIDES A VISUAL DISTINCTION BETWEEN THE TWO. THE KITCHEN IS ENTIRELY CONCEALED IN A STREAMLINED, CANTILEVERED WHITE CREDENZA UNIT (SHOWN BOTTOM LEFT).

APARTMENT 302

David Hicks

Melbourne

Australia

◄ A LARGE WHITE STORAGE UNIT SEPARATES THE LIVING AREA FROM THE BEDROOM, PROVIDING PRIVACY WITHOUT CUTTING OFF THE FLOW OF LIGHT.

► THE SLEEK BATHROOM IS LINED WITH SEAMLESS STAINLESS-STEEL CLADDING.

raised platform. With the existing slab concrete ceiling maintained, a linear bulkhead houses services and provides a strong visual link between the dining and living areas. To interrupt the flow of space, Hicks introduced a raised floor finished in black gloss paint, an unexpected gesture that reinforces the seductive, bachelor pad nature of the environment. A small study is incorporated into the entrance hall, which also doubles as a guest bedroom complete with fold-out bed.

All materials were commissioned as large panels, on a bigger scale than is usual for a domestic interior. This concept was carried through into the bathroom, which is lined seamlessly in stainless-steel cladding. The six metre (20 foot) wide white roller blinds, made from exterior building screen material, add to the theatrical nature of the space.

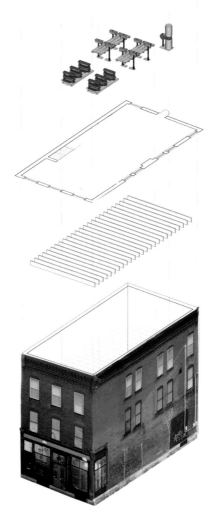

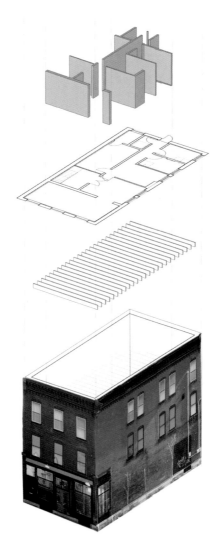

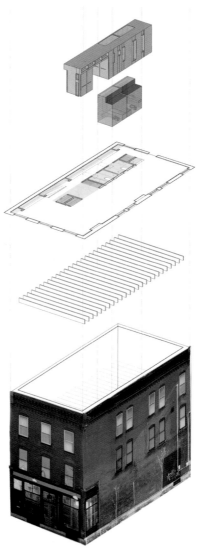

1870
Light manufacturing
Large open space with machinery

1930
Converted to housing
Small rooms

2005
Housing
Large open space with living machinery

312 LOFT
Studio for Architecture

Buffalo, New York

USA

STUDIO FOR ARCHITECTURE chose to design its ideal family space in a three-storey, red-brick warehouse in Buffalo, New York. The 1870s building had the advantage of windows on three of its four elevations. However, a conventional domestic refurbishment in the 1930s had produced awkward circulation spaces and bedrooms without natural daylight. The plan was to open up the two floors and convert the building back to its original state, restoring the structure and spaces, while creating a functional place to live.

Built to house light industry, the building has a shop on its ground floor that has been turned into the architects' studio. The 1930s conversion had carved into the beams to run the basic services. All the infrastructures embedded in the floor were removed and the free-span beams patched and repaired. It was decided that all domestic services, such as the bathrooms, laundry room and storage area, would be concentrated in 'container' structures. These would then be slotted into the infrastructure wall, which would house the plumbing, waste, ventilation, electrical and heating/cooling apparatus.

In keeping with the building's industrial history in which pieces of machinery were lifted into place, the architects chose to manufacture the bathrooms and laundry room off site as monocoque stainless-steel units that could be dropped into position. These units were manufactured to the minimum size allowable by

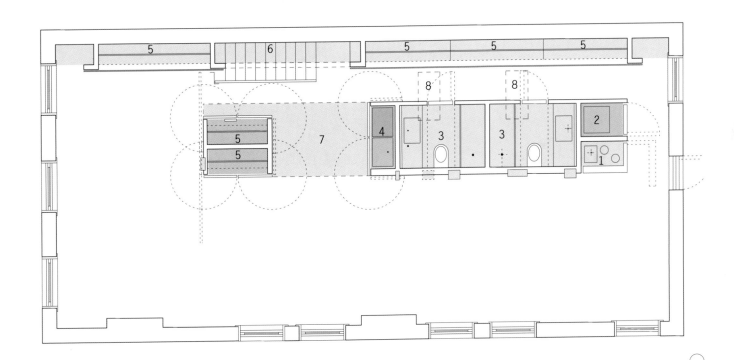

American building standards – 1.5 × 2.15 metres (5-7 feet) – with welded 14-gauge stainless-steel sheeting creating a strong industrial aesthetic. The architects describe the units as appearing much larger because of the spartan interior, the uniformity of the material and the light from the opening in the ceiling.

Measuring 1.8 metres (6 feet) wide, the container walls form an island that conveniently divides the foyer space and open-plan area. All the services are wall hung, dropped down from the ceiling and run vertically into a chase in the basement. This practical solution for all the living functions allows the island to be totally self-contained. Screened off, the open-plan space is uninterrupted so that furniture can float with no fixed arrangements. Not only does this permit total flexibility in how the space is used, but each day's changing light conditions may be freely observed. Extra storage space has been built into the party wall.

The third floor, which houses one large bedroom, still has independent access should a future owner want to return it to a single dwelling unit. It is a spacious living area that tracks the history of its interventions with coloured areas coding the changes: 'Every time that something was cut, we painted it a bright colour, hence the yellow ceiling, the blue wall, the green door' say the architects.

THE WOOD-CLAD INFRASTRUCTURE WALL HOUSES THE KITCHEN, BATHROOM AND OTHER SERVICES ON THE INSIDE, WHILE ALSO PROVIDING STORAGE ON THE OUTSIDE. BECAUSE IT IS FREE-STANDING IT ALLOWS FOR ENORMOUS FLEXIBILITY IN THE PLACEMENT OF FURNITURE AND USE OF THE SURROUNDING SPACE.

THE HISTORY OF THE development of loft living in Barcelona seems to mirror that of New York. Both cities underwent an economic boom fuelled by the introduction of light industry such as textiles and manufacturing in the nineteenth century. Light industrial warehouses sprung up in the downtown areas adjacent to the city's ports. But in Barcelona regeneration of these areas, after the buildings became redundant, has been slow. It was only when Barcelona was awarded the Olympics' contract in 1992 that the harbour and seafront underwent an urban regeneration project, bringing housing and tourists to the area.

Interior designer Cristina Rodriguez had been living a peripatetic existence fuelled by her desire to experiment with applying a plethora of styles to her various residences in Barcelona. After moving three times in six years, she focused her latest domestic experiment on a former textile factory situated on the edge of Barcelona's old town area. An L-shaped floor plan, comprising 200 square metres (2,150 square feet) of floor space, provided an ideal base on which to apply her notion of a romantic but functional apartment. The factory had lain derelict for almost a century, so the first task was to strip it bare of any services and remove all the plaster to reveal the original metal beams and decorative cast-iron columns. Rodriguez decided to create an open-plan area, only constructing walls to screen the master

◀ THE LIVING AREA IS SEPARATED FROM THE MAIN BEDROOM BY ONE OF ONLY TWO PARTITION WALLS IN THE APARTMENT – THIS ONE ALSO HOUSES A FIREPLACE.

▼ PLAN. 1. ENTRANCE. 2. GUEST BEDROOM AND BATHROOM. 3. OFFICE AREA. 4. LOUNGE FOR READING AND MUSIC. 5. KITCHEN/DINING. 6. LIVING AREA. 7. MASTER BEDROOM. 8. BATHROOM

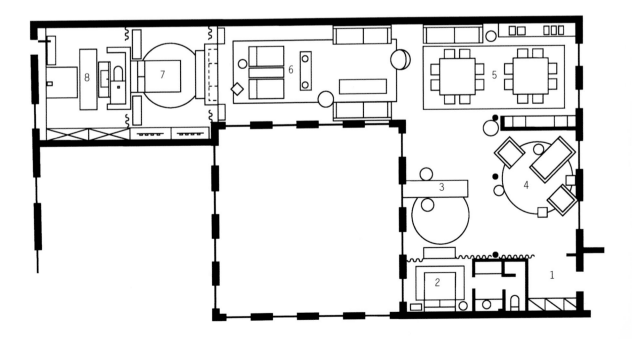

bedroom and bathroom. Elsewhere she has introduced curtains to create any temporary divisions required.

Within the principal living area, designated bays for eating, working and entertainment are denoted by furniture rather than by partitions. For the dining area, there is an industrial, stainless-steel kitchen unit and a rustic, solid oak kitchen table with high-backed chairs made by a local furniture designer.

The divider between the master bedroom and living space incorporates an open fireplace, while a lowered ceiling in the bedroom helps to create a sense of intimacy. For the bathroom, an Asian vibe is enhanced by tatami mats. Designed as a wet room, the concrete screed seals the floor and continues the industrial aesthetic.

▲ THE OFFICE AREA IS SEPARATED FROM THE GUEST BEDROOM BY A CURTAIN.

◄ THE DINING AREA AND KITCHEN BEYOND, WITH ITS INDUSTRIAL, STAINLESS-STEEL UNIT.

◄ THE POLISHED CONCRETE OF THE
BATHROOM IS COMBINED WITH
LUXURIOUS FURNISHINGS TO CREATE
AN EFFECT THAT IS BOTH INDUSTRIAL
AND ROMANTIC.

▼ A LOWERED CEILING CREATES A
SENSE OF INTIMACY IN THE MASTER
BEDROOM.

LONDON'S SHOREDITCH AREA was originally known for its concentration of furniture makers who produced intricate veneered cabinetwork and marquetry. Then it became run-down and depopulated, except for a few workers' cafés and a smattering of underground clubs and late-night bars. However. Shoreditch has fast gathered pace as one of the most fashionable creative neighbourhoods in London. A rash of interior-designed bars and the arrival of the White Cube gallery in Hoxton Square – promoting young British artists – confirmed the area's achingly cool status. Many of the light industrial warehouses have been converted into loft spaces, frequently with no trace of the building's original character. Instead cash-greedy developers have carved up the buildings to produce cavernous 'loft-style' apartments. Arguably, the area is a victim of its own success.

A Berlin-based practice set up in 2003, magma architecture has an expertise in developing strong concepts for urban sites and designing temporary structures such as the pPod, an aluminium framed tent for the Horse and Bamboo Theatre, Manchester's travelling theatre company. For the loft in Shoreditch, magma was asked by the clients, a young couple from France and Italy, to maximize the living space within the existing shell of a 175 square metre (1,884 square foot) rooftop apartment located on Great Eastern Street, in the centre of Shoreditch.

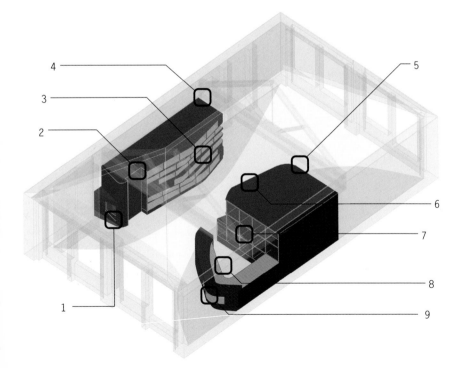

◄ DIAGRAM OF THE SOFTWALL UNITS: 1. CRYSTAL DISPLAY, 2. DOOR TO STAIRS DOWN, 3. BOOK LIGHT, 4. COAT CLOSET, 5. AMBIENT LIGHT, 6. BATHROOM DOOR, 7. COOKING COUNTER, 8. BAR COUNTER, 9. BOTTLE DISPLAY

EAST LONDON LOFT

magma architecture

London

UK

▲ THE DOUBLE-HEIGHT SPACE
FEATURES A MEZZANINE LEVEL, WHICH
IS SUSPENDED FROM THE BUILDING'S
EXISTING TIMBER TRUSS.

▲ THE KITCHEN AND BATHROOM ARE HOUSED IN THE MAIN 'SOFTWALL' UNIT AT ONE SIDE OF THE SPACE.

◄ THE KITCHEN 'SOFTWALL' CURVES AROUND TO FORM A BAR FOR GUESTS AND PROVIDE SEPARATION FROM THE DINING AREA.

▼ OFFSET CURVES ON THE OUTSIDE OF THE BATHROOM SOFTWALL UNIT EMIT AMBIENT LIGHT INTO THE LIVING AREA. THE SPIRAL STAIRS LEAD UP TO THE MEZZANINE.

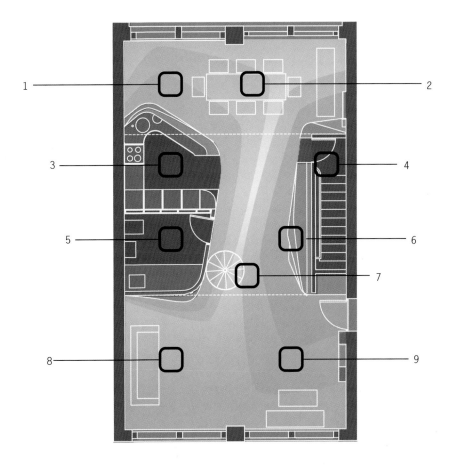

Magma designed compact containers, which they term 'softwalls'. These blur the distinction between furniture and walls and integrate the kitchen, bathroom and stairs. The dynamic form of the softwalls opens up a connection between the back area and street front, creating a continuous living space. This includes a kitchen, and the kitchen worktop area incorporates a bar. A secret door to a wardrobe is imbedded in the wall layout. At the lower level, the stair that leads down from the sleeping area is integrated within a backlit wall of books. The surfaces of the container walls are laminated in stained, birch-faced 8mm flexi-ply on timber studs, while kitchen appliances and worktops are laminated in stainless steel. For the client, the only requirement was to keep the existing mezzanine level but free up the open plan living area. To do this the steel columns that supported the 35 square metre (377 square foot) mezzanine have been removed and the floor is now suspended from the existing timber truss with additional support from steel plates.

R-H LOFT

Vincent Van Duysen Architects

New York

USA

THE BELGIAN ARCHITECT Vincent Van Duysen's immediate reaction on viewing the Manhattan loft situated between Greene and Prince Street, located in New York's Soho district, was to be charmed by the space: 'It has the expanse and spectacular views and the sort of unique roof tops that set New York apart from any other city.' Van Duysen created a dramatic interior reminiscent of the film noir genre within which his client, a young entrepreneur, could enjoy his urban lifestyle. At the same time, the loft is designed to provide a place of seclusion away from the pulsing energy of New York.

Vincent Van Duysen Architects specializes in the execution of minimalist interiors, architecture and furniture, describing its work as 'reductionist design pursuing primary forms and compact volumes'. A common language of symmetry and formalism can be seen running through its work, which focuses on retail and domestic architecture.

The conversion of the vast 500 square metre (5,380 square foot) industrial space into an apartment reflects its former industrial state with black-painted, cast-iron columns and restored original features such as the air-conditioning ducts suspended from the corniced ceilings.

Re-using loft space came into fashion in the 1950s, when lofts were often converted in an ad hoc way that reflected the inhabitants' lifestyles, generally a

▾ THE LIVING AREAS ARE AT THE
BOTTOM OF THE PLAN, WITH THE
BEDROOMS AND BATHROOMS AT THE
TOP. WHILE THE LIVING AREAS ARE
OPEN-PLAN, THE REST OF THE ROOMS
FOLLOW A MORE TRADITIONAL,
CELLULAR LAYOUT.

bohemian set who lived on limited incomes. By contrast, Van Duysen's loft is designed to an extremely high standard of detailing. The client wanted a space that would be both dramatic and masculine, a far cry from New York's other housing stock, the brownstone terrace. In setting the mood of the space, the architects were influenced by Rex Stout, the American detective writer responsible for the cult detective figure Nero Wolfe.

In terms of conventional loft living the property is unusual in that, instead of supporting a series of open plan living spaces, it has a traditional domestic layout of cellular rooms. This was the choice of the client who wanted a sequence of smaller rooms in contrast to the large living space. The living area is divided into different zones, that of day and night. With direct access from the entrance hall, it accommodates space for living, dining and cooking and a corner for preparing quick meals. The six windows that span the entire façade give spectacular views over the city.

The furniture takes on an architectural language, helping to define the zones. A dining table that seats up to twelve people is complemented by a light sculpture, which hangs from the ceiling and helps to contain the space. On the other side of the living area is the library with concealed bookshelves, large, leather ottomans and two Barcelona chairs.

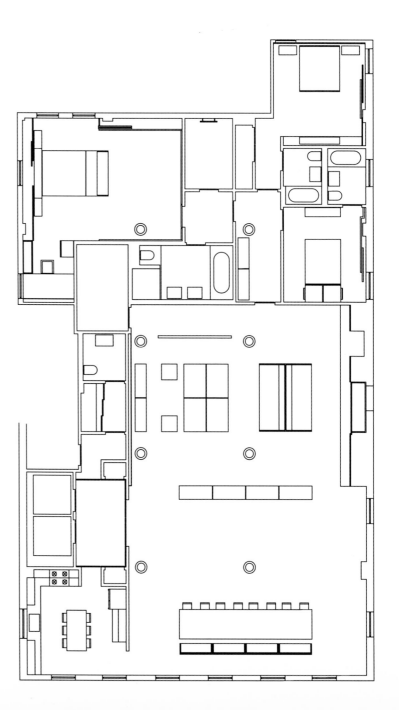

▲ VIEW FROM THE LIVING AREA ACROSS
TO THE DINING AREA. THE LOFT'S
ORIGINAL CAST-IRON COLUMNS
AND AIR CONDITIONING DUCTS –
RESTORED AND PAINTED BLACK –
ARE CELEBRATED AS ARCHITECTURAL
FEATURES.

◄ THE DINING AREA, WHICH SEATS UP
TO TWELVE PEOPLE, IS ILLUMINATED
AND DEFINED BY A LIGHT SCULPTURE
SUSPENDED ABOVE IT.

▲ THE LIBRARY AND READING SPACE
SITS TO ONE SIDE OF THE MAIN
LIVING AREA.

From the living area, a corridor leads to the master bedroom and two guest rooms. The master bedroom resembles a Peter Greenaway film set. With heightened proportions, the space is almost entirely painted in dark hues that shift from grey to black. There are no wardrobes but a self-contained storage space concealed behind sliding doors adjoins the bedroom. In the guest bedrooms a dramatic contrast is created with rich red walls and dark timber bedheads forming a screen, behind which sits a pair of graphic white chairs from the 1960s.

Dark oak floors have been introduced throughout while white-painted window surrounds are used to frame views of the city. The overall effect is one of genuine simplicity, overlaid with a level of detailing that displays a mastery of controlled function.

▲ IN THIS RED-PAINTED GUEST
BEDROOM, A SCREEN BEHIND THE BED
HIDES TWO CHAIRS AND A DESK.

◄ THE MASTER BEDROOM – DECORATED
IN HUES RANGING FROM GREY TO BLACK
– INCORPORATES A SMALL WORK AREA
IN ONE CORNER.

PATRICK TIGHE ESTABLISHED his practice after working as an associate at the Santa Monica-based Morphosis, one of America's most experimental and investigative practices. This experience helped him to develop a strong individual aesthetic.

Tighe was asked by his client – a creative professional – to convert the warehouse shell that he had acquired in downtown Los Angeles. The 130 square metre (1,400 square foot) space was to provide a sanctuary from the city's 24-hour culture and a place in which to live, work and entertain.

The design sets up a distinct dialogue between the angular geometry of the stone-clad spa platform and the free-flowing, organically shaped kitchen pod. Through these two divergent forms a series of counterpoints emerge. The sculptural entities flow, entwine and overlap, creating a dynamic interior.

The client's brief was for a space with state-of-the-art technology that would allow him to view his collection of abstract photographic images on a digital display media wall. The wall of video monitors serves as an extension of the client's computer desktop. Situated in the principal space, the media wall is used for viewing films and photography and for gaming, as well as a virtual art gallery. Technology is integral to the environment – the ambient lighting, heating and audiovisual settings are all controlled from a central station.

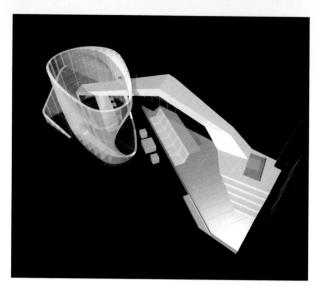

▲ COMPUTER-AIDED DESIGN WAS INTEGRAL TO THE EXECUTION OF THE SPACE'S COMPLEX GEOMETRIES.

▼ PLAN OF THE LOFT. 1. KITCHEN, 2. MEDIA WALL, 3. WORKSTATION, 4. SPA, 5. RAISED DECK, 6. FIREPLACE, 7. LIVING AREA, 8. BATHROOM

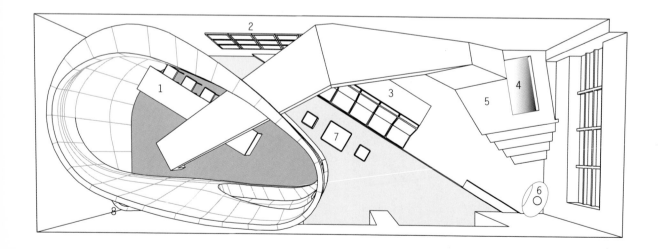

LIVE/WORK LOFT
Tighe Architecture

Los Angeles, California

USA

◄ THE ORGANIC FORMS OF THE KITCHEN POD (LEFT) CONTRAST WITH THE ANGULAR GEOMETRY OF THE STEPS AND PLATFORM OF THE SPA AREA (RIGHT).

▼ THE ARCHITECT WORKED CLOSELY WITH THE CLIENT, PRESENTING COMPUTER SIMULATIONS AT EVERY DESIGN STAGE, FROM CONCEPT TO CONSTRUCTION.

Tighe developed the scheme in close collaboration with his client, presenting three-dimensional computer simulated models throughout to ensure the client could engage with every stage of the design, from concept to execution. Working with such complex geometries meant that the forms had to be designed using a computer model and fabricated using a CNC (computer numerically controlled) milling process.

A raised floor of translucent panels allows for the LED lighting system below to morph from one colour to the next. This floor continues into a seating formation providing a sofa and workstation. Building materials were chosen for their ability to absorb or reflect the desired colours.

Stone steps rise to the platform of the stone-clad monolith, which has a raised deck where the spa is situated, daringly close to the workstation. The in-house spa incorporates an air-bath tub, a stylized 'garden' and a floating steel fireplace. Natural light flows in from the main façade window behind.

The kitchen is composed of undulating curved walls that form a womb-like enclosure. A 4.5 metre (15 foot) stainless-steel work bench with seating area compliments the futuristic forms. Finally, in a witty take on the bohemian chic of open-plan lofts, where privacy is minimal, the bathroom is thinly concealed behind the pod's skin as it is peeled apart to make room for the toilet and hand basin.

4

RADICAL

SEATRAIN RESIDENCE
Office of Mobile Design

Los Angeles, California
USA

◄ THE SEATRAIN RESIDENCE IS A FINE EXAMPLE OF LA FREESTYLE ARCHITECTURE - A LARGE PERCENTAGE OF THE BUILDING'S MATERIALS WERE RECLAIMED FROM THE NEIGHBOURING ARCHITECTURAL SALVAGE YARD.

▶ THE SITE IS LOCATED IN ONE OF THE CITY'S LARGEST LIVE-WORK ARTISTS' COLONIES. THE ARCHITECTS WERE GIVEN PERMISSION TO BUILD ON TWO THIRDS OF THE SITE.

▼ THE ARCHITECTS PLANTED LUSH TROPICAL PLANTS AND DESIGNED A STREAM THAT PUMPS WATER AROUND THE SITE.

OFFICE OF MOBILE DESIGN was formed to explore the concept of mobility and how it could be applied to the static world of architecture. A transportable educational eco laboratory, Mobile Eco Lab, is one example of such a project. By designing structures that rest lightly and temporarily upon the land, OMD is rethinking and re-establishing methods of building.

In downtown Los Angeles, Office of Mobile Design created the Seatrain residence which 'literally grows up from the land around it'. The site is adjacent to Brewery, the 300-strong live-work units, which make up one of one of the largest live-work artists' colonies in the United States. The client, Richard Carlson, a developer and co-owner of the Brewery worked closely with the architects, holding daily site meetings to plan the house as it was being built.

The bold industrial aesthetic of the 300 square metre (3,230 square foot) residence is a result of selecting industrial building components and steel containers from the Los Angeles scrap yard that neighbours the site. These recycled materials are symbolic of the industrial past of downtown Los Angeles and, from them, a fine example of LA freestyle architecture has been pieced together. The house includes exotic elements such as a 10 metre (32 foot) koi fish pool with a glass bridge that runs parallel to the living space. Salvaged grain trailers are transformed into a lap pool, while large storage containers are used both to

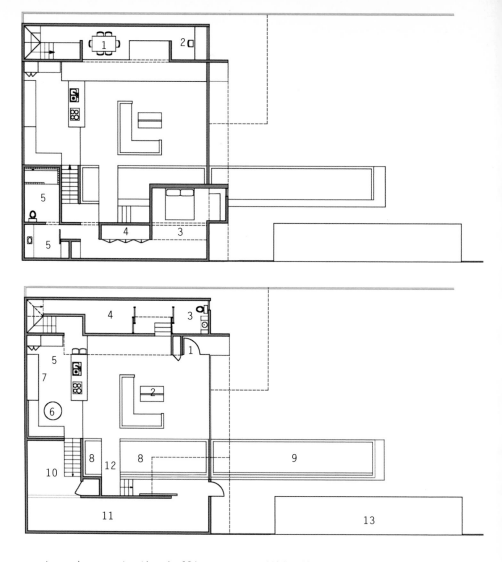

create and separate the dwelling spaces within the
house. Each storage container has an individual function: one is the entertainment and library area,
another is a dining room and office space overlooking
the garden below, a third serves as the bathroom and
laundry room and a fourth is the master bedroom. This
is a visually dramatic, protruding volume that wraps
around the upper part of the house. The industrial
aesthetic creates a dynamic interplay of forms and
materials - contrasting corrugated metals, industrial
containers and exposed wooden beams - against the lush
background of the tropical garden.

▸ IN THE MAIN LIVING AREA A SHEET OF 22 MILLIMETRE (¾ INCH) TOUGHENED GLASS SPANS THE WATER CHANNEL WHICH LEADS INTO THE KOI FISH POND.

▾ THE KITCHEN IS INTEGRATED INTO A WORKSTATION THAT HOUSES ALL THE SERVICES AND DOUBLES AS A BAR AT WHICH TO EAT.

▴ THE DOUBLE-HEIGHT LIVING AREA IS OVERLOOKED BY THE OPEN UPPER-LEVEL OFFICE.

▲ THE 'SHIELD' BUILDING ATTACHED
TO GASOMETER B. COOP HIMMELB(L)AU
WERE THE ONLY ARCHITECTS TO ADD AN
EXTERNAL VOLUME TO THEIR
DEVELOPMENT.

▼ PLAN OF A TYPICAL HOUSING LEVEL
IN GASOMETER B, WITH THE SHIELD ON
THE RIGHT.

ments and offices. The 360 apartments offer diverse configurations from three-bedroom split-level apartments and loft apartments to smaller studio accommodation intended for students. The apartments, which average 77 square metres (828 square feet) are accessed by a central circulation core.

All four gasometers are linked at the ground-floor level via the shopping mall. Inside Gasometer B the mall creates a spatial and functional buffer between the event hall and the apartment/office wing, therefore intensifying the internal communication. The sky lobby on the sixth floor provides a social space for the residents.

Manfred Wehdorn, an architect known for his work in the area of restoration, was invited to renovate Gasometer C and create 92 living units. The architect based his design on three principles: the clear order of new functions, the creation of the highest possible living quality and a simple architectural language that created an understated dialogue with the existing structure. Situated within the area of the former water reservoir, the programme provided five storeys of parking and two storeys of retail and entertainment at the level above the conical embankment directly connected to the other gasometer buildings by bridges. Above this rises the new, central construction with its three office floors and six residential floors, forming a ring around the

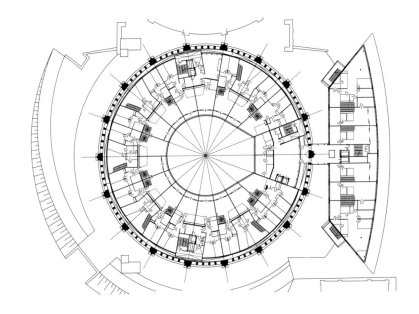

▾ SECTION THROUGH GASOMETER B,
WITH THE SHIELD TO THE RIGHT.
THE MULTI-LEVEL VOLUME OF THE
EVENT HALL CAN BE SEEN AT THE
BASEMENT LEVEL.

▸ DETAIL OF THE MID-LEVEL STEEL
BRIDGE THAT LINKS THE SHIELD
(LEFT) TO THE ORIGINAL BUILDING
(RIGHT) OF GASOMETER B.

▸▸ THE SHIELD, WHICH CONTAINS
HOUSING AND OFFICES, LEANS TOWARD
THE ORIGINAL GASOMETER AT THE
LEVEL OF THE LINKING BRIDGE, AND
THEN DRAMATICALLY KINKS AWAY AS
IT EXTENDS UPWARDS.

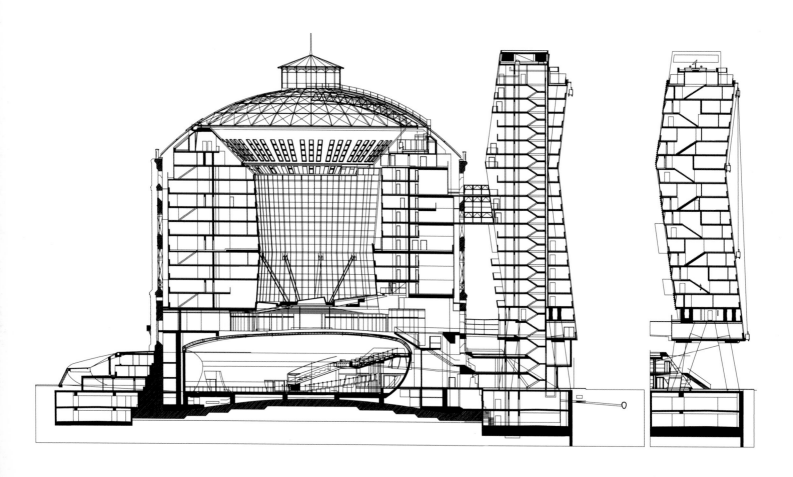

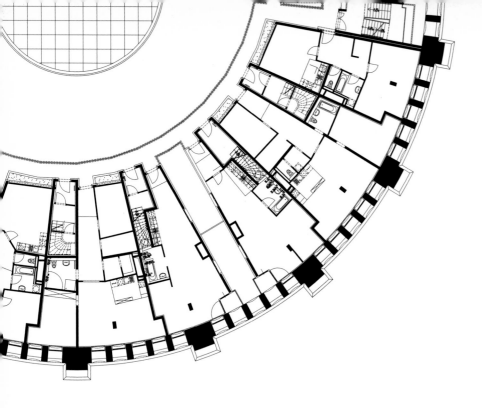

◄ PART-PLAN OF A TYPICAL HOUSING
LEVEL IN GASOMETER C. EXTERNAL
WALKWAYS CONNECT THE APARTMENTS
ON THE INNER FAÇADE, CREATING A
COMMUNAL OUTSIDE SPACE FOR
RESIDENTS.

▼ THE INNER RING OF GASOMETER C
CONSISTS OF A MODERNIST, WHITE-
RENDERED FAÇADE OF STEPPED
TERRACES THAT TAPER AS THEY REACH
THE UPPER LEVELS.

inner wall of the historical gasometer building and tapering upwards creating stepped terraces. In addition, the new construction is broken down vertically into six segments - in the spaces between the towers there are four stairwells and two open spaces which give a view of the historical structure of the building and act as additional light apertures for the new residential court. The two top storeys are occupied by maisonettes with their own private terraces. The success of the project is the creation of small, intimate external areas that counteract the grand scale of the building, as a result of the formation of six vertical towers and additional small inner courtyards, which adjoin the historical outer wall. The interior has been designed with a simple formal language and rendered in white. The architect describes the design as a contemporary reading of the classical Viennese residential houses designed by Adolf Loos. The inner courtyard is richly planted - a system has been installed to collect rainwater for watering the green zones, with a separate system for collecting both drinkable and non-drinkable water for residents.

Wilhelm Holzbauer's treatment of Gasometer D incorporates 126 dwellings as well as offices for the city archives and communal gardens. Unlike the first three gasometers (which all have central open atria with living and office space around the inner edge),

▲ THE THREE-WINGED LAYOUT OF
GASOMETER D ALLOWS FOR THREE
SEPARATE GARDENS (AT THE HOUSING
LEVEL) FOR THE USE OF RESIDENTS.

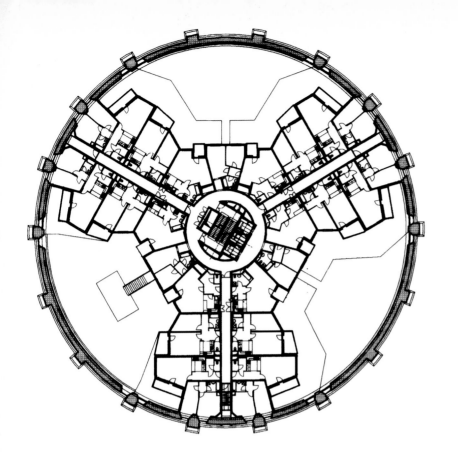

Holzbauer's programme consists of a central circulation core, off which protrude three wings. The spaces in between the wings accommodate the gardens, with atria above. In this way, much of the original inner walls and their window openings are still visible. The three wings are white, rendered modern blocks with balconies overlooking the gardens.

A series of entrances enables the gasometers to function for evening activities as well as providing public spaces for daytime use. The foyer of the event hall in Gasometer B is connected to the 'night mall', thus becoming a transit area for those using the hall. The development's mixed-use approach creates a place that accommodates round-the-clock activity: working, living and entertaining.

Summing up the project, Coop Himmelb(l)au's Wolf Prix outlines the position of conservation and how it can play a role in the contemporary environment: 'Vienna's history shows that monuments are not sacrosanct buildings but vital elements of a dynamic city. Besides the main centre situated on the Danube, the Gasometer project is a second local urban centre creating a tension between the city's historical core and new developments. This tension enables the dynamic developments every city thinking about its future needs. Density is urbanity. We are proud that this theorem on urbanity has also been acknowledged in Vienna.'

▴ PLAN OF A TYPICAL HOUSING LEVEL IN GASOMETER D. UNLIKE THE OTHER THREE GASOMETERS, WHICH CONSIST OF A RING WITH A CENTRAL ATRIUM, HOLZBAUER'S DESIGN INCORPORATES THREE WINGS THAT RADIATE FROM A CENTRAL CIRCULATION CORE.

◂ AERIAL VIEW OF GASOMETER D.

▸ SECTION THROUGH GASOMETER D. THE CENTRAL CIRCULATION CORE REACHES ALL THE WAY TO THE TOP OF THE GASOMETER.

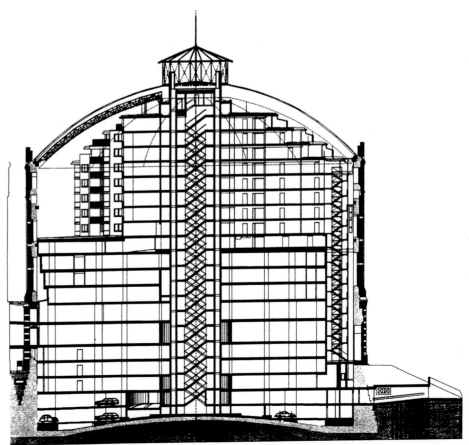

CHELSEA RESIDENCE

Lacina Heitler Architects/The Apartment Creative Agency

New York

USA

REM KOOLHAAS'S RETROACTIVE manifesto on New York, *Delirious New York*, published in 1978, forecast the state of urbanism and urban lifestyles, siting a scenario for twentieth century living at the Downtown Athletic Club, New York, where naked boxers would stand on the ninth floor eating oysters at the bar with boxing gloves on. This prediction may have been a little extreme, but he was right in saying that sporting facilities would take on a 'lifestyle' element.

The YMCA, which for almost 100 years served as a safe haven for thousands, providing lodgings, social activities and spiritual support, has moved its premises to a modernized facility. Left vacant, the old YMCA building has been converted into a set of stunning apartments. The duplex is perhaps indicative of New York's rich and diverse culture. The building has featured in fascinating episodes of New York's history. Established in 1869, it was the first YMCA in New York City. Its pool was used as a backdrop for the first meeting between Edmund Lynch and Charles E. Merrill, which changed the world of investment forever. In 1972, the building's steam rooms were used as the film set for the 'disposing' of Mo Green in Francis Ford Coppola's *The Godfather*.

The 650 square metre (7,000 square foot) luxury residence, which incorporated a running track for YMCA members, is testimony to the wealth and demand

▲ ESTABLISHED IN 1869, THE MC BURNEY YMCA WAS THE FIRST IN NEW YORK CITY. THE ORIGINAL RUNNING TRACK (SHOWN IN THIS PHOTO TAKEN BEFORE CONVERSION) IS SUSPENDED FROM A SERIES OF STEEL TRUSSES OVER THE BASKETBALL COURT.

▶ IN THE UPPER-LEVEL FORMAL DINING ROOM, VERNER PANTON CHAIRS SURROUND A DINING TABLE DESIGNED BY THE INTERIOR DESIGNERS, THE APARTMENT.

for unusual living quarters in New York. The Chelsea Residence is a rarity, with five bedrooms and bathrooms, two home theatres, and a reception area that incorporates the original running track with its nine metre (30 foot) ceiling and giant overhead trusses, from which the running track was suspended.

Lacina Heitler Architects, a New York-based practice, and interior design firm The Apartment Creative Agency were keen to keep the integrity of the building and the spirit of its very particular past. The basketball court, which has the running track hovering above it, now incorporates the 'great room'. The old signage, which stated '20 laps equals one mile' is now covered by the plasterwork but the lines of the court were painstakingly recreated. Wherever possible the original floorboards, laid more than 50 years ago, have been retained. A single-run staircase leads up to the running track with a clear glass balustrade, which runs the perimeter of the track, allowing natural light from the east and west facing windows into the space. The dividing wall between the great room and master bedroom houses the gas fire and plasma screen. Zebrano wallpaper creates an exotic wood effect, and the colour scheme evokes Italian pop art with the steel beams of the original structure painted fuchsia pink and complemented by a lime green sofa.

◂ THE MASTER DRESSING ROOM IS
DESIGNED AS A GLAMOROUS BOUDOIR,
WITH WALLPAPER BY TIMOROUS
BEASTIES ON THE CEILING AND
A DISCO MIRROR BALL.

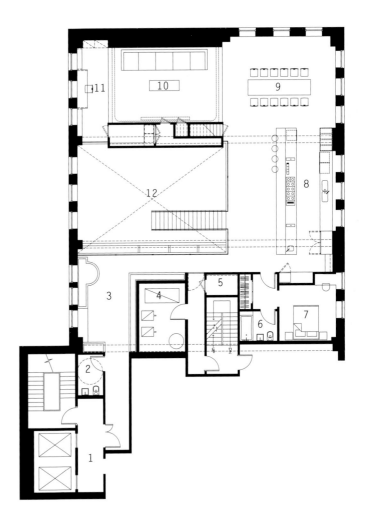

▲ LOWER-LEVEL PLAN. 1. STAIR,
2. BATHROOM, 3. ENTRANCE,
4. MECHANICAL ROOM, 5. LIVING
ROOM, 6. MASTER BEDROOM,
7. MASTER BATHROOM, 8. MASTER
CLOSET, 9. BEDROOM, 10. DESIGN
ROOM

▲ UPPER-LEVEL PLAN. 1. ENTRANCE,
2. WC, 3. GARDEN, 4. MECHANICAL
ROOM, 5. CLOSET, 6. GUEST
BATHROOM, 7. GUEST BEDROOM,
8. KITCHEN, 9. FORMAL DINING
ROOM, 10. HOME THEATRE,
11. OFFICE, 12. VOID

▶ THE L-SHAPED, UPPER-LEVEL
'GARDEN' HAS BUILT-IN CONCRETE
PLANTERS FOR YEAR-ROUND GREENERY.

The master closet, which accommodates a large shoe collection, makes use of the only space in the duplex that has no views.

On the second floor level one reaches what is fashionably named the 'über-kitchen'. At 7.3 metres (24 foot) long, the kitchen is a larger than most cooking areas found in the average restaurant, and features a planted indoor garden with grow lights. The kitchen counter, made from white Corian with moulded sinks, acts as a bar and preparation area. Lacina Heitler describe the area 'as a theatre set, to include the chef in all social activities while cooking and entertaining'. For preparing a more modest snack, there are also two kitchenettes.

The duplex is also for serious entertaining. On the ground floor there are two receiving rooms and a home theatre with computer controlled audio/video system. A mezzanine bedroom is accessible through a secret door, and affords the best observation position in the duplex to view the evening's social activities.

▲ DESCRIBED AS AN ÜBER-KITCHEN, THE AREA IS LARGER THAN THAT FOUND IN MOST RESTAURANT KITCHENS. THE 7.3 METRE (24 FOOT) LONG CORIAN WORK SURFACE TAKES CENTRE STAGE.

▶ THE BOLD COLOUR SCHEME OF THE LOWER-LEVEL, DOUBLE-HEIGHT LIVING ROOM IS ACCENTUATED WITH ZEBRANO WALLPAPER AND THE FUCHSIA-PAINTED STEEL COLUMNS.

◄ THE CONTAINER UNITS WERE
ORIGINALLY USED AS ACCOMMODATION
FOR WORKERS IN THE OIL INDUSTRY.

▼ THE UNITS WERE STACKED AND
ROTATED TO CREATE A MULTI-FACETED
FAÇADE.

B-CAMP

Helen & Hard

Stavanger

Norway

HELEN AND HARD BOTH STUDIED in Oslo but decided to base their practice outside the capital, in the northern city of Stavanger, because they received a string of commissions from the city and because Stavanger's planning laws - more liberal than Oslo's - meant more freedom to build and procure commissions. The architects' approach to design encompasses a social agenda that often leads to a fresh programme of usage and a more dynamic and active relationship between client and architect. In 2004 they were commissioned to convert workmen's huts into five flats and ateliers and in the same year transformed an old brewery into a cultural centre. They describe their design philosophy as 'discarding any a priori imposed values, instead concerning themselves with design that can liberate specific forms to inspire participation and experimentation'. In 2003 the practice purchased an area of land adjacent to their studio, situated on the riverfront that forms part of an urban regeneration programme in the east of Stavanger. The once thriving Norwegian oil industry has collapsed and one of the greatest challenges is what to do with the leftover infrastructure. Helen & Hard proposed the project - which they named B-camp and described as an incubator - and bought a number of containers formerly used as workers' accommodation units. These were reconfigured on site to provide low-rent studio accommodation. Each unit provides between 25 to 35 square metres (270 to

▶ THE CONTAINER UNITS WERE CRANED INTO POSITION ON SITE. EACH DWELLING IS MADE UP OF TWO UNITS.

◀ FROM LEFT: PLANS OF THE LOWER AND UPPER LEVELS. GREEN AREAS INDICATE THE COMMUNAL COURTYARD. THE STUDIO IS AT THE TOP OF THE GROUND-FLOOR PLAN.

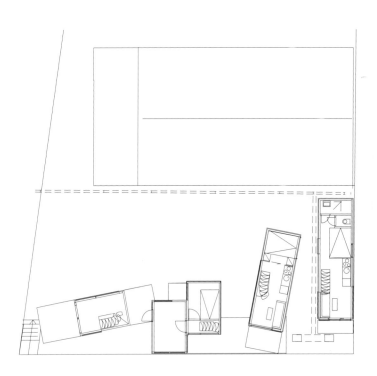

377 square feet) and forms part of a larger site programme that offers such amenities as a common
courtyard and access to the Helen & Hard studios,
equipped with a workshop, model-making facilities and
conference rooms.

The units were craned into site, with two standardized units used to make up each dwelling. By stacking
and rotating the units the architects have created an
interesting configuration for a new urban typology. The
relatively small living area is compensated with
higher than usual floor-to-ceiling heights, split-
level spaces and individual terraces on the upper
level. Part of the architects' philosophy is to
recycle materials, and in this project the units are
clad with surplus windows and doors - scrap materials
from the metal industry. A transparent, corrugated
plastic panel (which provides an insulating effect
necessitating only 5 centimetres/2 inches of extra
insulation for a satisfactory u-value) was applied as
an external skin. Many of the tenants have personal-
ized their façades by introducing materials such as
laser-cut sheet steel or slate tiles. The properties
have become so successful that there is already a
waiting list and talk of repeating the model in other
areas of the city.

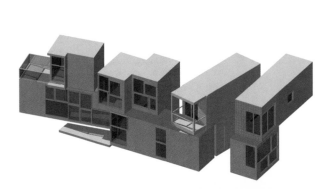

▸ COMPUTER MODELS SHOWING THE
IRREGULAR, ROTATED POSITIONING OF
THE VARIOUS CONTAINERS.

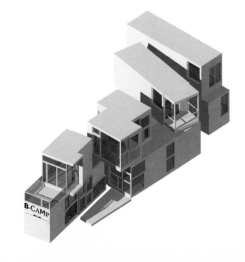

Laurence King Publishing
Ltd have paid DACS'
visual creators for the
use of their artistic
works.

Emma O'Kelly would like to thank Mark, Alfie and Matilda.

Corinna Dean would like to thank Alan and Fidelity for their general guidance and Liz Faber at Laurence King for all her assistance.

The publisher would like to thank Adam Hooper of Hoop Design and research coordinator Fredrika Lökholm.